INDIA-PAKISTAN

PARTITION PERSPECTIVES IN INDO-ENGLISH NOVELS

INDIA-PAKISTAN

PARTITION PERSPECTIVES IN INDO-ENGLISH NOVELS

By

V. Pala Prasada Rao

M.A.., M.Ed., M.Phil.

Lecturer in English

Jagarlamudi Kuppuswamy Chowdary College

Guntur–522 006

Editors

Prof. K. Nirupa Rani

M.A., Ph.D.

Department of English

Andhra University

Visakhapatnam

&

Dr. Digumarti Bhaskara Rao

M.A., M.Sc., M.A., M.Ed., Ph.D.

Reader and Research Director

R.V.R. College of Education

Guntur–522 006

Andhra Pradesh

D P H

DISCOVERY PUBLISHING HOUSE

NEW DELHI-110002

Published by:

Tilak Wasan

DISCOVERY PUBLISHING HOUSE PVT. LTD.
4383/4B, Ansari Road, Darya Ganj
New Delhi-110 002 (India)
Phone : +91-11-23279245, 23253475, 43596065
E-mail : discoverypublishinghouse@gmail.com
sales@discoverypublishinggroup.com
web : www.discoverypublishinggroup.com

Edition: **2020**

ISBN: 978-81-7141-766-7

India-Pakistan: ***Partition Perspectives in Indo-English Novels***

Printed at:
Infinity Imaging Systems
Delhi

To

those who stood for
human dignity
during the partition tragedy

Preface

History as the theme of creative fiction seems to cast a spell over many an Indo-English novelist. Writers, who surfaced after independence, generally reflect either the freedom struggle or the ultimate attainment of independence with a critical attitude, bringing the darker aspects that made a mash of the struggle. It can be said that this attitude is imbued with a spirit of nationalism. The purpose of such criticism is to learn lessons from the past for the betterment of one's attitude of mind. In fact, 'consciousness of the bad is an essential prerequisite to the promotion of the good'.

In August 1947, the sub-continent went off at a tangent from the unique ideal of non-violence as people started wallowing in bouts of communal mayhem. The decision of the British to partition the sub-continent into two separate nations—India and Pakistan—led to one of the ghastly orgies of violence the world has ever seen. Like the ravages of the medieval plague a mania for murder swept across the face of northern India and Pakistan for six terrible long weeks. The Muslims, on the one hand, and the Sikhs and the Hindus, on the other, callously butchered one another. In that swift splurge of slaughter over quarter of a million people were done to death and many more lakhs of people rendered homeless. Communal frenzy caused huge exodus of population on both sides.

There are a good number of writers for whom partition is the matrix of the plots. However, Khushwant Singh's *Train to Pakistan*, Chaman Nahal's *Azadi*, Bhisham Sahni's *Tamas* and Bapsi Sidhwa's *Ice-Candy Man* have been chosen for the thematic study of partition-theme. These novels have been chosen not in a haphazard fashion but with an intention to encompass different perspectives on partition, juxtapose the sensibilities of the novelists, and appreciate their impressions within the framework of the dissertation. *Train to Pakistan* is included for it is the first Indo-English novel on partition with its realistic portrayal of the upheaval. *Azadi* tries to capture the whole gamut of variegated issues involving in partition 'in epical dimensions.' The inclusion of *Tamas* needs a note of elaboration. Originally written in Hindi, it is translated into English by Jai Rajan. It has been regarded that the spirit of the original is carried into the English version. This novel is significant because it tries to expose, without mincing matters, the falsity of communal leaders and their Machiavellian ruses to grab power—the supposed cause of partition. It may be said that the three novels are the mouthpieces of Indian novelists' versions on partition. It is, therefore, inferred that at least one novel reflecting a Pakistani perspective on the trauma would make this study more comprehensive and varied, and this in fact entails the inclusion of *Ice-Candy Man*.

This book is divided into six chapters. The first chapter, 'An Historical Perspective of Partition', offers an evaluation of some important themes relating to the Muslim separatism and its growth and how this has culminated in partition. The aim is to unfold the breakdown of inter-communal networks which had, for so long, kept intact the social fabric of Indian society and probe into a larger historical question: Why did secular nationalism fail to realise a united India?

The subsequent four chapters, named after the novels, are intended to study the thematic paradigm of partition-theme in all the four novels. In the second chapter, *Train to Pakistan*, an attempt has been made to trace the process of disintegration of social mores which is consequent upon the degeneration of harmonious relations. In the third chapter, *Azadi*, the primary concern, as evidenced in the novel, is to show that partition was the result of the leaders' collective failure and the Britishers' studied indifference to ease up communal tangle. *Tamas* evinces the novelist's main thrust, the all-pervasive influence of communalism and the self-styled leaders' pre-occupation with it during the pre-partition times and how they have bungled important issues at a crucial point of time which ensued the parting of ways. In the fifth chapter, *Ice-Candy Man* has been chosen to study minority complex which was set in motion by a long chain of closely nested, mutually interlocking actions. Nevertheless, sincere attempt is made to study certain frame of references—co-existence, interdependence, communalism and its pernicious results, the disintegration of values, national leaders' incompetence and inability to iron out their differences with regard to communal problem, the divide-and-rule policy of the British and their manoeurvres, the novelists' diatribe against two-nation theory, the horrors of partition, the baffling problems of the refugees and the novelists' use of technique in the artistic expression—which form the essential ingredients of this thesis. The last chapter sums up the generalizations that have been inferred.

Partition novels are necessarily preoccupied with the past, yet literature is contemporary in its relevance and related to the problems of the present. The undertone of all these novels is to convey a powerful message to guard against communalists of all hues, and this modest study seeks to expose the scheming communal leaders who were hell-bent on generating and fomenting conflicts on communal lines and offer insights into the true colours of the divisive forces that whipped up communal frenzy. Chaman Nahal says: 'I feel the true horror of partition deserves to be read more systematically so that there are no further partitions in the sub-continent.' In fact, there is a greater need to understand how the tragedy of partition played itself out, understanding its nuances, its moment through the keen study of literature proper which might help redefine and reshape contemporary society. The purposive study enables one to comprehend the past politics and perhaps at the same time the mind-boggling contemporary communal politics. In fact, the thematic content and emotional overtones of these novels are essentially artistic exercises in the form of cathartic expiation of communalism.

Pala Prasada Rao
Bhaskara Rao

August 15, 2003
India's Independence Day

Contents

An Historical Perspective of Partition

Works on literature do [illegible] me into existence autonomously. They are [illegible] d with a number of social, cultural, economic, histo[illegible] political factors. It is these factors which help in the understanding of the genius, form and content. The partition novels are triggered off by an event invested with historical importance. So an historical perspective of, and an insight into, partition will help to understand the novels on partition better. So the historical perspective is intended to cover the tumultuous decades which witnessed the rise of nationalism and the growth of communalism.

The partition of the Indian sub-continent in 1947 is one of the great tragedies the magnitude of which compels one to search for the larger meanings. So many of those who lived through the trauma of partition were unable to comprehend how a nation, built around certain common symbols and shared ideals was so easily fragmented. So many more could scarcely understand why their dream of a united and secular India was destroyed by religious fanaticism.

The roots of Pakistan can be traced in the pre-British period, but its full germination took place on the eve of the British departure from India. Reflecting on the whole gamut of events at the time of independence and partition, social scientists often reiterate the view that the partition holocaust in 1947 was the crown and consummation of British machinations, the culmination of a separatist process initiated by a colonial government to foster and promote its imperial interests. But not all agree to this indictment. Some subscribe to the view that Pakistan came into being because Muslims constituted a separate nation and their animosity with Hindus started long before the British surfaced on the scene. 'Hindu-Muslim antagonism', states a proponent of this view, 'was embedded in the historical logic of India. Britain only witnessed it; she did not create or exaggerate it.' The evolution of 'Muslim nationalism,' so runs the argument, was linked with an independent demand of a 'nationality' apprehensive of its political future.

Muslim separatism, its birth, development and character have been a major theme in modern historical writings. Many views have been put forward regarding the causes that have paved the way to Muslim separatism culminating in partition.

There has been a welter of opinions regarding the commencement of Muslim separation. The Simla Conference marked 'a breakwater in Indian political history,' wrote Maulana Abdul Kalam Azad. He has observed:

> It was the first time that negotiations failed, not on the basic political issue between India and Britain, but on the communal issue dividing different Indian groups.[1]

There is no gainsaying the fact that Simla Conference marks a definitive parting of the ways between Hindus and Muslims. But the communal issue was far from being a new element in Indian politics in 1945. Some authorities on history have looked on the failure of Congress to form coalition ministries in 1937 as the turning point in relations between the two communities. Others go back to 1928, when All Parties' Conference rejected separate electorates. Some see Jinnah's departure from the Congress in 1921 as the point of no return; and others go back to the birth of the Muslim League in 1906. But whatever date is accepted as marking political breakwater, it is certain that the communal problem goes back much further to a time when there was no political life as such in India.

Hindu-Muslim relations during the first of millennium of Muslim rule in India can be studied in the light of two different methods of 'Islamisation' of India pursued by the Muslim rulers: One was the assimilation or the accommodation of Hindu culture; and the other was of confrontation and liquidation. Akbar, who has been acclaimed as 'benevolence' personified, was the one who initiated the former type. Being a crafty statesman, he saw the necessity of accommodation between Hinduism and Islam for the stability and prosperity of the country as well as his empire. He acquiesced to the Hindus by marrying Hindu women, raised the Hindus to the highest position, and finally proclaiming himself as the spiritual leader of the world. His new religion, Din-illahi, was intended to strike a harmonious chord between Hinduism and Islam. It is mentioned in *Ice-Candy Man* that emperor Akbar 'invited Zarathushti (Parsi) scholars to his darbar.' He even expressed his wish 'to become a Parsi if he could' which speaks volumes of his religious tolerance. However, the death of Akbar saw probably the death of accommodation and compromise.

The process of Islamization of India through confrontation and liquidation of Hindu culture began as early as 711 A.D. when Muhamad Bin Qasim, during his invasion of Sind, circumcised Brahmins by force and killed those who resisted. As India was dar-al-harb—a territory ruled by the non-Muslims— the liquidation process had a great appeal to the Muslims. Further, the failure of Akbar to evolve a Hindu-Muslim synthesis led to a greater triumph of the liquidation under his grandson, Aurangzeb, who attempted to make his empire a dal-al-Islam, an abode of Islam. His rule was characterised by destruction of temples and images, reimposition of the jiziah tax—a tax imposed on non-Muslims—replacement of Hindu officials by Muslims and the prohibition on the celebration of the Hindu festivals led to discontentment among the Hindus. In his seminal work, Pakistan—The Formative Phase, Khalid bin Sayeed has remarked that 'perhaps Emperor Aurangzeb was responsible for increasing Hindu-Muslim tension by trying to Islamicize the Moghal government...It is also true that Maratha and Sikh rulers raised their banner of revolt against him because in trying to organise his government on Islamic lines, the emperor was acting against their interests.' Touching upon the same issue in a general fashion, Balbir K. Punj in his article, 'Healing Achilles Heel (in *Outlook*, November 2002) says: 'for varied reasons, temples have been Hindus' Achilles' heel all through the Islamic age in India. The annals of the Delhi Sultanate are full of attacks on 'Kafiresque' Hindu temples, often on festival days.' However, the policy of tolerance was followed in the states that sprang up during the decline of Mughals. The first Dewan of Haidar Ali was a Hindu; the Sikh ruler Ranjit Singh had two Prime Ministers, one a Muslim and the other a Dogra Hindu. Akbar Shaw, father of Bahadur Shaw-II, used to tell his ministers.

> If you Mussulmans are to me like one eye, truly the Hindus are dear to me like the other eye.[2]

Hindus and Muslims fought together during the Revolt of 1957 against the British. Much of the strength of the Revolt lay in Hindu-Muslim unity. The Hindu and Muslim rebels respected each other's sentiments. For example, wherever the Revolt was successful orders were immediately issued banning cow-slaughter. However, after the suppression of the Revolt, the British government had taken a particularly vindictive attitude towards the Muslims, hanging 27,000 Muslims alone. Muslims were looked on with suspicion. Annoyed at the intense hostility of Muslims to British rule, the Britishers made up their minds to enfeeble Muslims in such a way that they would not rise again. They discriminated against them. The Persian script was replaced by Devanagari, and Urdu by Hindi. No foreign power can rule any country without the support of at least a section of indigenous population, and the British were busy modelling their educational and administrative policies with an intention to woo the Hindus, keeping Muslims in the chilly wilderness of suspicion—as has been pointed out—and neglect. Advertisements in the press inviting applications for government posts in those days, as a rule, made it abundantly clear that the vacancies would be given only to Hindus, thus excluding Muslims completely from government service. Commenting on the misery of the Muslims Dr. Pattabhi Sitaramayya in his *History of Congress* remarked that the 'nobility, particularly the Muslim nobility, was practically crushed out of existence and there was not even a titular person left to serve as a rallying point in any future adventure like that of 1857.'

But around 1875 there was a reversal of British policy. The Hindus had learned their lessons 'a little too well.' In education, business and the professions, it was Hindus who broke new ground. The Muslims stagnated, unwilling to embrace the ways of the conquerors. The time had come to set right the balance as 'Hindu nationalism' was gaining momentum.

One of the first steps the British took to rally the Muslims was to patronize the Muhammadan Anglo-Oriental College of Sayyid Ahmed Khan. This institution provided the impulse for the Aligarh movement, which not only fostered a Muslim cultural renaissance, but also encouraged the sense of Muslim separatism.

In his early life, Sayyid Ahmed Khan took a broad-minded view of communal relations. But in his concern for the betterment of his community, Sir Sayyid was easily persuaded that democratic institutions would result in the permanent subservience of the minority community. He tried to prevail upon the British to look upon Muslims with sympathy rather than contempt, and at the same time beseeched the Muslims to profit by their recent experience to take whole-heartedly to western education, which was the key to their progress, in the changed circumstances. He propagated the view that it was futile to challenge the British rule in India; it was accepted as a reality. The Urdu-Hindi controversy made him dubious of Muslims' interests in the first instance. When a Muslim, Badr-al-Din-Tyabjee was elected as the leader of the Indian National Congress in 1887, Ahmad Khan emerged actively in opposition to it. In his view, "Hindu-Muslim alliance could only be disadvantageous to the Muslim community which was smaller in number, educationally backward, politically immature and economically insecure."[3] Alliance with the Hindus against the British could only lead to the loss of the British patronage. Therefore, he discouraged Muslims from joining the Indian National Congress, and looked on the British administration as the protector of Muslims' interests.

The British did nothing to discourage this view. They had good reason to encourage disunity between the Hindus and the Muslims. A handful of foreign officials were in charge of a population numbering hundreds of millions. The rulers depended as the last resort on an army in which Indians outnumbered the Europeans two to one. They could survive largely due to their successful playing off one community against the other. In *Tamas*, Richards confides in to his wife, Lizza, that the 'ruler is safe when people are fighting among themselves. The history of British rule in India offers many examples of this strategy of 'Divide and Rule.' This advocacy is strengthened by no less an authority than Lord Elphinstone, the Governor of Bombay, who wrote in his minute of 14th May, 1859: "Divide *et impera* was the old Roman motto; and it should be ours.' In the twentieth century alone there were the partition of Bengal, the engineering of the Muslim deputation, the wrecking of the Unity Conference of 1932, and many other acts. The motive behind their special favour to Muslim League was, what a retiring British Secretary of State called' "a predominant bias in British officialism in India in favour of the Muslim community, partly on the ground of closer sympathy, but more largely as a make-weight against Hindu nationalism."[4] The English rulers decided to put themselves between the Hindus and Muslims so as to create a communal triangle of which they would remain the base. Addressing the problem and the diabolical role played by the British, Gandhi has rightly remarked: "This quarrel is not old; this quarrel is coeval with the British advent." In other words they began to encourage communal and separatist tendencies in Indian politics. For this purpose they decided to come out as the champions of the Muslims. It is not without reason Col. Bharucha, Parsis' leader in *Ice-Candy Man,* squarely blames the British for all the problems because they are 'pastmasters of intrigue'. The British watched the two communities fighting because it was easier to rule a house that was hopelessly divided.

To make matters worse, the strong Hindu tinge in Congress leadership's thought, propaganda and agitation through ideas associated with Hindu religion tended to repel and alienate Muslims instinctively. So many Congressmen of stature were closely associated with revivalist movements. The cow protectionists in Punjab were very generally Congressmen. Madan Mohan Malaviya was the moving spirit behind the Hindu revitalization movement. He was connected with the Prayag Hindu Samaj, the Sanatan Dharm Mahasammelan and the Shuddhi Sabha. He forged close links with those influential groups who shared his undaunting enthusiasm for Shuddhi, Sangathan (which were aimed to convert non-Hindus into Hindu fold), Hindi, the cow and the Hindu Maha Sabha. Referring to this phenomenon, Dr. Pattabhi Sitaramayya admits that all these movements were really so many threads in the strand of Indian nationalism and the nation's unity was to evolve a synthesis so as to be able to dispel prejudice and superstition, to renovate and purify the old faith (Hinduism), the vedantic idealism, and reconcile it with the nationalism of the new age. The Indian National Congress was destined to fulfil this great mission? Thus many a Congress leader of name and fame equated nationalism with more of less religion. Gandhi, for instance, writing in *Young India* in 1931, made the following remarks; 'Cow protection is an article of faith in India. Apart from its religious sanctity, it is an ennobling creed. It is the dearest possession of a Hindu heart...No one who does not believe in cow-protection can possibly be a Hindu."

Gandhi is considered the greatest advocate of peace and Hinduism's creed of non-violence. 'He was a deeply religious man but his Hindu dharma was inclusive not exclusive. Ram and Rahim, Ishwar and Allah, Buddha and Nanak, Tulasi and Kabir, were never far from his heart' to quote Natwar Singh's article 'Remembering Gandhi'.

In this direction, Gandhi really catered to the new secular national consciousness. Still, his political thought was couched in the language of religiosity. The best example of his use of a religious symbol was his interpretation of independence as Ram Rajya. He ardently made all efforts for the protection of cows though his ideas on it were different from other communal versions. So too his definitions of non-violence and truth were steeped in Hindu religious traditions. His notion of 'spiritualising politics' and 'inner voice' also tended to create a religious aura around politics. Some people had misgivings about the inner voice. In his celebrated work on Jinnah,

Prof. Waheed-Uz-Rahman has castigated that 'Gandhi was an enigma and a sort of mystic who seldom spoke directly and mostly acted on impulse which he conveniently described as his inner voice. Even apart from Gandhi, other leaders like Subhash Chandra Bose and the general run of Congress workers freely used Hindu symbols, myths, imagery and idioms. This Hindu tinge created "general unrest, panic and doubt' and 'an atmosphere of fear and suspicion' among Muslims, especially in the northern India. The Muslims were convinced that under the leadership of Gandhi, 'a non-violent violence-monger' as the butcher in *Ice-Candy Man* puts it, 'the liberation of Hinduism will benefit the Hindus only' and that 'the Muslims can feel free only in Pakistan."[5] In his article in the *Comrade* entitled 'Communal Patriot' Mohammed Ali wrote in 1912.'

> The spectacle of a go-ahead Hinduism, dreaming of self-government and playing with ancient gods in the vesture of democracy dazed the conservative Muslim...He felt as if he was being treated as an alien, as a meddlesome freak, who had wantonly interfered with the course of Indian history. With the loss of empire, he felt as if he were to lose his self-respect as well. The 'communal patriots' amongst Hindus treated him as a prisoner in the dock, and loudly complained of him as an impossible factor in the scheme of India's future.[6]

The secular aspects of the national movement led by the Congress were also distorted by several other features. A large number of nationalist leaders assumed a dual socio-political role within the circle of their co-religionists. Till early 1930s, several leaders were simultaneously members and leaders of the Congress and the Hindu Mahasabha. In the novel, *Tamas,* it is seen that Lakshmi Narain and Mehtaji have 'one leg in the Congress and the other in the Hindu Mahasabha.' By the time the Congress strategy was modified in the mid-1930s and "its leaders were awakened to the reality of a communal monster, the opportunity of forging independent links with the Muslim masses was lost."[7]

Most of the nationalists among Muslim youth did not fully accept the modern secular approach to politics. The result was the most important issue they took up was not political independence but protection of the holy places and the Turkish Empire. Even during the Non-Co-operation Movement thousands of Muslim peasants had attempted to leave India, a non-Islamic land, and cross over into Afghanistan. The heroes and myths and cultural traditions, which they regarded in high esteem and awe, belonged not to ancient or medieval Indian history but to West Asian history. V.S. Naipal says:

> A convert to Islam changes his view of the world. His holy places are in another country. His sacred language is Arabic. He rejects his own history and turns away from his own historical background'[8]

Their habit of looking at political questions from a religious viewpoint turned out very detrimental to the India-in-making.

The Muslims were also convinced that there was the age-old enmity between Hindus and themselves. Hindus were dangerous because they were ungodly people, kafirs. As long as "he does not profess the right religion he will remain our enemy. To kill a kafir brings merit,"[9] runs the argument of a Muslim in *Tamas*. This sort of religious frenzy does not augur well for a united India.

The separatist tendencies among a section of the educated Muslims and the big nawabs and landlords reached a climax when the All-India Muslim League was founded to become the first platform of Muslim interests. It preached that the interests of the Muslims were different from those of the Hindus. The Muslim League's political activities were directed not against the foreign rulers but against Hindus and the National Congress. It was thus played into the hands of the British who announced that they would 'protect and advance the political rights and interests of Mussalmans in India.'

None of the ominous implications of the British to safeguard Muslim's rights was lost upon the Viceroy, Lord Minto, who was behind the Minto-Morley Reforms. The real purpose of the Reforms was to divide the nationalist ranks and check the growing unity among Indians by encouraging the growth of communalism.

The League's success in obtaining concessions from the government encouraged Hindu fundamentalists to establish an organisation seeking the interests of their own community. An all-India Hindu organisation, Hindu Mahasabha, took form during the second decade of the 20th century. The result was an increase in communal tensions. Thus it caused deep fear and distrust in the minds of the Muslims. Nehru has rightly reflected:

> To some extent this fear is justified, or is at least understandable in a minority community...A special responsibility does attach to the Hindus in India both because they are the majority community and because economically and educationally they are more advanced. The Mahasabha, instead of discharging that responsibility, has acted in a manner which has undoubtedly increased the communalism of the Muslims and made them distrust all the more. ...One communalism does not end the other, each feeds on the other and both fatten.[10]

Hindu organisations were harping on the theme of Muslims' ungodly nature and their antagonistic ways. In *Tamas,* Vanaprasthaji chants a couplet in order to prevail upon the audience about 'the sins of the Muslims in the land.' In their bid to confront the villainous Muslims they adopt such measures like using stick and other deadly weapons which adversely heighten communal consciousness.

As perception of reality dawned on both sides and with the commencement of non-violent Non-Co-operation Movement, the spirit of sacrifice infected all. Organised non-co-operation with the British fostered spontaneous co-operation between Muslims and Hindus. Members of the two faiths demonstrated together and lived together in British jails. One happy result was a lessening of communal tension.

Another agitation that welded Hindus and Muslims was the Khilafat Movement. Britain meted out harsh treatment to Turkey after its defeat in the First World War. Indian Muslims were outraged over this attack on the integrity of their religion. A Khilafat Movement was started to recapture the Turkish Sultan's dominion, the Caliphate (called Khilafat in India).

Gandhi embraced the cause of his Muslim fellow-countrymen. He saw that the movement provided an opportunity for uniting Hindus and Muslims. Ali brothers and Azad, leaders of the movement, introduced Gandhiji to the Muslim masses. Cries of 'Hindu-Musalman-ki jai' and 'Hindu-Musalman ek hai' resounded through the air. Jinnah, suspicious of Gandhi's mass following, declared that the new leader drew his principal support from 'inexperienced youths and the ignorant and illiterate.' So saying, Jinnah withdrew from the Congress.

The collapse of the Non-Co-operation Movement in the mid-twenties marked the end of joint political action by Hindus and Muslims. The Muslim League, which had been overshadowed by the Khilafat Committee, again became prominent. Its leader, Mohammed Ali Jinnah, who once called himself an 'Indian first and a Muslim second' became a fervent opponent of the Congress.

Jinnah's position as the leader of his own community did not go unchallenged. Upset by the independent stance of Punjab's Muslims, he spent the years 1930 to 1935 in London. Summoned back to India after the passing of the Government of India Act, he braced himself for the final fight.

While politicians were arguing over the details of the safeguards to be written into India's future constitution, some Muslims outside the political arena began to formulate more ambitious demands. In 1930, the great poet, Sir Muhummad Iqbal, addressing the Allahabad session of the Muslim League, declared: "The formation of a consolidated North-West India Muslim State appears to me to be the final destiny of Muslims"[11] in that region. Iqbal did not specify that this state would be independent of India. This element was introduced later, when his idea was taken up and expanded by some young Muslims studying in England. Chaudhury Rahmat Ali, the leader of these students, proposed, in pamphlets of 1933 and 1935, the creation of a separate Muslim nation in North-West India. It would be called Pakistan, from the first letters of Punjab, Afghan Province (NWFP), Baluchistan. When Rahmat's idea was presented to the Muslim delegates of the Joint Select Committee, they condemned it as an impractical 'students' scheme.' Even Jinnah told him that it was 'an impossible dream.' Still he had been acclaimed as 'the best ambassador of Hindu-Muslim unity.' But as relations between Hindus and Muslims degenerated, the idea caught on.

As Indian leaders failed to draft a constitution to which all parties would agree, the British government took an initiative to draft a constitution known as the Government of India Act, 1935. In April 1936 the Congress and the League, meeting separately, decided to contest the elections held according to the new Act. The Congress had swept the polls. It won absolute majorities in five provinces and was the largest party in four others.

The only provinces remaining outside the Congress orbit were Punjab, Sind and Bengal. Interestingly none of these provinces, all of which had a Muslim majority, went to the League. The League had in fact fared rather badly in the elections, winning only 109 of the 482 seats reserved for Muslims. Even the Congress, which had contested only 58 of these seats, won 26 of them.

Despite his party's poor showing, Jinnah, the perennial President of the League, suggested that Congress-League coalitions should be formed in several provinces. Some efforts were made to arrive at an agreement, particularly in the United Provinces, but League leaders ultimately refused to accept the terms proposed by the majority party. Congress leaders thought a link-up with the League could "knock over the British government which had relied so much on those (Hindu-Muslim) troubles." But Jinnah chose to stress the differences; and Congress, after its landslide victory, felt it had no need of the League's support.

Jinnah took the Congress position as a direct bluff. He accused Gandhi of 'turning the Congress into an instrument for the revival of Hinduism' and of wishing to 'establish Hindu Raj in the country.' Stating that the Muslims would never get a fair deal from the Congress of the Muslims he began persuading people. "For the classes he preached the western doctrine of national independence, the two-nation theory. For the masses he hammered on the danger of Hinduization and Hindu provocations."[12] The growing tensions between the two communities were driving more and more nationalistic Muslims into the hands of Jinnah. In less than a decade, this sowing of distrust would bear fruit for everybody was bent on 'jockeying for power,' to quote Colonel Bharucha, in *Ice-Candy Man*.

When the Congress came to power it imposed its own party anthem *Bande Mataram* ('Hail to thee, Mother) as the official new anthem of government in callous disregard of the feelings of Muslims. Muslim Leaguers attacked it on the ground that it was 'positively anti-Islamic, idolatrous.' They also maintained that it had been composed in the Anand Math by Bakim in an anti-Muslim context. Many Congress leaders saw that while the attack was basically communal, there was also some substance in it. Nehru, after reading Anand Math, wrote to Subhash Chandra Bose in 1937 that the background of the song was likely to irritate the Muslims. "There is no doubt that the present outcry against *Bande Mataram* is to a large context a manufactured one by the communalists. At the same time there does seem some substance in it and people who are communistically inclined have been affected by it."[13]

Yet Congress leaders failed to rectify the situation fully; they did drop all but the first two stanzas for Congress use in 1939 partially because of the pressure of a section of Congressmen. Interestingly, the rectification came, though rather late, in 1947 in independent India.

Thus instances of 'continued oppression in small ways'—as Lord Linlithgow puts it—made Muslims line up behind Jinnah, their Quaid-i-Azam or Great Leader. When he called for the observance of a 'Day of Deliverance and Thanks-Giving' after Congress ministries resigned in 1939, his followers did not fail to respond.

The resignations, necessary as they might have been from the point of ideology, deprived the Congress of the political advantage it had enjoyed since 1937. The ministries of Bengal, Punjab and Sind did not resign. When the government looked to Jinnah for support he 'made the very most of the situation'. Divisive tendencies that had gradually been increasing were now given an open expression.

The stage now was set for the fatal demand. It came on 24 March 1940, at the Muslim League's annual session at Lahore. A resolution was passed calling for the grouping of 'geographically contiguous units' in areas where Muslims predominated, such as north-western and eastern India which would form 'independent States in which the constituent units shall be autonomous and sovereign.' The language was vague, and deliberately so. Were the League's leaders pressing for a looser confederation? Or were they simply bluffing, hoping to scare the Hindus, and the British, into granting more extensive concessions? Or were they really thinking of cutting the country in two, creating a new Muslim state? The Lahore session asked for 'adequate effective and mandatory safeguards' for Muslims in areas of the country where they were in a minority.' Hidden in this demand lies one of the greatest defects of the whole idea of Pakistan.

The Lahore resolution came as a surprise departure from the previous Muslim League ideology and shocked Indian nationalists. It was based on the theory that there were two nations in the Indian sub-continent. This became the anchor of Muslim League policy from that time on. The demand for Pakistan, in terms of political expediency, was based on the inability of the political parties involved to chalk out a common programme to go by. At that time, nevertheless, the demand for Pakistan was not taken seriously either by the Congress or others. It was looked upon mainly as indicative of Jinnah's hardening stance.

The vision of a separate homeland began to cast a spell on Indian Muslims. 'It brought back to them a longing for the Moghal empire and all that was glorious in it.' (Pakistan by Damodar P. Singhal). It seemed to the rank and file of Muslims as an escape from Hindu oppression and exploitation. The rich Muslims saw a promise in it, a rare opportunity to make fortunes without fierce competition of the Hindu mercantile community.

The idea of Pakistan is incongruous because more than a third of India's Muslims lived in Hindu-majority areas that could never have become parts of a separate Muslim state. Yet it was through the support of these Muslims that the League gained strength to partition the country.

At the time of the Lahore Resolution, the League was strong precisely in areas where Muslims were in a minority. In provinces where they predominated—the North-West Frontier, Punjab, Baluchistan, Sind, Bengal—they had no use for the excessive demands of the League. In these provinces ministries had been elected that were responsive to the needs of the local population—Muslim, Hindu or Sikh. They did not want to have anything to do with Pakistan. The whole idea was 'undesirable even from the Muslim point of view,' declared Sir Sikandar Hyat Khan, Unionist premier of Punjab in 1941.

Later, however, the League grew in strength in the Muslim-majority provinces. The League conquered the bulk of the middle class as well as the lower class. By 1942, Jinnah actually assumed a position like Gandhiji so far as Muslims were concerned and thence Pakistan dominated the political discourse. Increasing communal pressure, aggravated by the clamour raised by Hindu communalist groups, drove moderate Muslims into Jinnah's camp. Encouraged by its growing strength the League adopted a new slogan in 1943 'Divide and Quit.' It was a sad alteration of Gandhi's intrepid battle cry to the year before. From this point onward the shadow of Pakistan hung over the Indian nation.

Meanwhile, the Second World War in Europe was continuing. Late in March 1941 Churchill sent Sir Stafford Cripps, a socialist member of the War Cabinet, to negotiate on the government's behalf with Indian leaders. His proposals promised 'the earliest possible realization of self-government in India'. Most parties doubted the truth of Britain's declared intention to share executive power. Furthermore, the clause that permitted provinces to secede from the proposed union was, in the eyes of Congress leaders, 'a severe blow to the conception of Indian unity' for it admitted the possibility of a separate Muslim state. Muslim leaders felt that the mere possibility was not enough. They claimed that partition was 'the only solution of India's constitutional problem.' The Cripps Mission failed to deliver the goods.

After the failure of the Cripps Mission, Rajagopalachari, the Congress leader of Madras, concluded that the only way to break the communal deadlock was to accept the League's demand for a separate state. Though his proposals were turned down, Rajaji did not give in. In 1943, while Gandhi was in jail, he discussed a scheme with him a scheme which would serve as a basis for a settlement with the League. A year later, after Gandhi had been released, Rajaji communicated his formula to Jinnah, saying that it had Gandhi's 'full approval.' Gandhi no doubt approved of the formula insofar as it might provide the basis for fruitful discussions. But he latter made it clear "that he really did not believe in it, and that what he wanted was some form of self-determination for Muslims in a United India."[14]

The Rajagopalachari formula went much further than this. In exchange for the League's endorsing 'the Indian demand for independence' and pledging co-operation 'with the Congress in the formation of a provisional interim Government,' it in effect accepted the League's Lahore resolution. It added that 'contiguous districts would be demarcated in the north-west and east of India, wherein the Muslim population is in absolute majority.' Here plebiscites would be held on the basis of adult suffrage or some other just basis in order to 'decide the issue of separation from Hinduism.' Any transfer of population would be 'on an absolutely voluntary basis.'

These proposals, however, improved Jinnah's bargaining position rather than to be taken seriously. Kanshi Ram, in *Azadi*, is historically conscious when he has remarked that the Rajaji formula 'put the idea' in Jinnah's head. For him, it is the heart of the whole issue of partition.

After the failure of talks based on Rajaji's formula, Lord Wavel designed a plan to ease the present situation and to advance India towards her goal of full self-government. A conference was held in the summer capital, Simla, to which leaders of the Congress, League, Sikhs, Scheduled Castes and other groups were invited. The main topic of discussion would be the formation of a new Executive Council. This meant, as Secretary of State, L.S. Amery, explained that Britain was 'placing India's immediate future in Indian hands.'

The Simla Conference began on a note of optimism. Gandhi, who had opposed to the Cripps offer, felt that Wavell's plan was sincere and would lead to independence. Jinnah, however, 'flatly refused to co-operate,' as Wavell later reported. He was determined to undermine the Conference unless it agreed to his own terms. These included the demand that the Muslims not belonging to the League could not be appointed to the Executive Council. Congress President, Abdul Kalam Azad, firmly opposed any such arrangement. Himself a Muslim, Azad was well aware that 'a large bloc of Muslims had nothing to do with the League.' The Congress would be betraying its Muslim members if it accepted Jinnah's demand.

Wavell would not proceed without obtaining Jinnah's co-operation. When it was withheld, the Viceroy announced the failure of the Conference. Jinnah had in effect been given the power to veto overall the negotiations, and he would use or threaten to use this weapon again and again in the months to come.

In England, Labour Party came to power. It had long been pledged to the establishment of self-government in India. Now it had a clear majority in Parliament and so it could carry out its promises.

The Viceroy announced that elections to the central and provincial legislatures would be held within a few months in August 1945 and have decided to establish Executive Council with the support of the main Indian parties. The results were announced in December. In the Provincial contests, the Muslim League won almost all the reserved Muslim seats. The Congress also fared well in the general electorate. The League managed to set up ministries in Bengal and Sind. In Punjab it was forestalled by a coalition of Unionists, Akali Sikhs and the Congress. The central elections followed the same pattern. India's Muslims entrusted their fortunes to the League; the rest of the country was solidly behind the Congress.

As all India seemed to be filled with a spirit of discontent and daring, Britons were in a fix. Economically shattered and weary after six long years of war, Britain's interest in its empire had waned. So the government announced the sending of the Cabinet Mission to unravel the constitutional deadlock.

To tide over the impasse, the members of the Cabinet Mission began to hold meetings with the leaders. The Mission issued a statement containing its own proposal on 16 May 1946.

The foundation of the Cabinet Mission Plan was an undivided Union of India, which would consist of all the British Provinces and Princely States. The idea of Pakistan was rejected. The Mission was convinced that the creation of a separate state would not solve the communal problem and would besides be contrary to the wishes and interests of a very large proportion of the inhabitants of Punjab and Bengal. In addition, partition would create many serious problems in defence, communications, and other areas. The demands of Muslims could be met by granting complete autonomy to the various provinces. The federal government would look after foreign affairs, defence, communications and transportation; all other subjects would go to the provinces and state provinces were even given the right to opt out of the federation.

The Muslim League at first accepted the Cabinet Mission Plan in toto in the hope that it would ultimately result in the establishment of a complete sovereign Pakistan. The Congress accepted the long-term plan, but not the proposals for the interim government, since they would force the Congress to give up its 'national character' (by viewing it as a 'Caste Hindu party'), to 'accept an artificial or unjust parity' (Muslims were given disproportionate representation), and to 'agree to the veto of a communal group' (the League). Nevertheless the Congress agreed to join the Constituent Assembly.

The Cabinet Mission plan guaranteed the unity of India, runs the argument of Abdul Kalam Azad, while at the same time it held out the necessary assurances to the minorities. Indeed it promised to break the deadlock. The Muslim League subscribed to the plan; so did the Congress Working Committee. But on 10th July, 1946 Nehru in reply to a question posed by the press said that the Congress would enter the constituent assembly completely unfettered by agreements and was free to meet all situations as they arose. The Muslim League, it was evident, accepted the plan only under duress. Naturally Jinnah was not happy about it and was outraged at the statement. 'This would mean that the minorities would be placed at the mercy of the majority,' he remarked with a touch of bitterness.

It claimed that the Congress was 'bent upon setting up a caste Hindu Raj in India with the connivance of the British,' and demanded immediate establishment of Pakistan. In order to bring about this, it called upon the 'Muslim Nation to resort to direct action.' In *Azadi*, Kanshi Ram laments the leaders' failure to rise to the occasion so as to understand the efficacy of the Cabinet Mission Plan, which was the last desperate effort to stave off partition.

The League did not spell out what its intentions were, and in many places the day was marked by peaceful demonstrations of Muslim solidarity. But in Calcutta the situation quickly got out of hand. Encouraged by a conniving League Ministry, and undeterred by an irresolute British administration, bands of Muslim rowdies went on a rampage of looting, arson, rape, and murder. Hindus retaliated and for several days Calcutta was in a chaotic state. Thousands were killed, tens of thousands injured, lakhs left homeless, property worth crores of rupees destroyed. Not without reason this terrible episode is remembered as the Great Calcutta killing.

The communal contagion then spread to Noakhali and Tripura, where Hindus in minority were subjected to various indignities. When Hindus of Bihar heard of the outrages and forced conversions taking place in eastern Bengal, they decided to take revenge on the local Muslims. Mobs of 'ordinary peasant folk,' as Nehru later described them, were seized by some 'madness' and tried 'to exterminate the Muslims' of the area. Contained in one place, the infection broke out elsewhere. The United Provinces, Punjab and Bombay all contributed to the sum of horrors. Then the communal contagion spread across northern India. India was reeling towards a full-scale civil war.

In the midst of this man stood up for sanity and human dignity. He was Mahatma Gandhi who went to Noakhali in November and lived their until March 1947. 'The seventy-seven-year-old saint walked from village to village, begging shelter from the local Muslims, sharing their food and caring for them. The country was moved by the simple demonstration of Hindu-Muslim co-existence. 'The heroism, the tenacity and the will of simple people in actual life,' to quote Chaman Nahal,' far exceeds anything one can find in fiction! *(Across Borders)*.

The all-pervading communal frenzy and sectarianism had been reflected at Delhi where leaders were engaged in internecine quarrels. These did not cease even with the establishment of the Interim Government. The League joined in the government to fight for Pakistan. Jinnah declared that "the Interim Government should not be allowed to do anything which directly or indirectly prejudices or militates against our demand of Pakistan."[15] They refused to accept the leadership of Nehru. The business of the state came to a standstill.

In consonance with the Cabinet Mission Plan elections were held to the Constituent Assembly in which the League secured 90 per cent of Muslim votes. Towards the end of *Tamas* it is said with prophetic accuracy that 'no Muslim could win without League's support in the Muslim electorates in the days to come.' It became a reality in 1946 when the Muslim League secured 90 per cent of the Muslim votes. Democracy continued to divide the polity into opposing parties and set up periodic battles between them. In the process, neither victory nor defeat was permanent. Victors had to prove themselves and losers got a chance to redeem themselves.

Encouraged by its strength the Muslim League did not take part in the Constituent Assembly. It is obvious that something drastic had to be done to break the deadlock. The initiative was taken by Prime Minister Attlee who, on 20 February 1947, announced in Parliament that the government's 'definite intention' was to transfer power 'into responsible Indian hands by a date not later than June 1948.' This historic declaration caught everyone by surprise. Attlee also announced that Admiral Lord Louis Mountbatten would be replacing Lord Wavell as Viceroy.

At this juncture, Mountbatten came with instructions to work for a united India. Congress and Akali leaders were vehemently opposed to partition. But Jinnah was adamant. Mountbatten held six meetings with Jinnah. They agreed to one point at the outset—the need for the speed. According to Jinnah, India had gone beyond the state at which a compromising solution would be possible. There was only one —a speedy 'surgical operation.' Otherwise, he warned, 'India would perish.' When Mountbatten expressed concern that partition might unleash bloodshed and violence Jinnah reassured that once his 'surgical operation' took place, trouble would cease and India's two halves would live in harmony and happiness. When Mountbatten told Jinnah that India should remain united since partition was detrimental, Jinnah asserted:

> India has never been a nation. It only looks on the map. The cows I want to eat, the Hindu stops me from killing. Every time a Hindu shakes hands with me he has to wash his hand. The only thing the Muslim has in common with the Hindu is his slavery to the British.[16]

Jinnah touched upon the chord of religious feelings of the Muslims which acted as a rallying force in Muslim politics. He continued to harp on the differences insisting that Muslims were a nation with a distinctive culture and civilization, language and literature, art and architecture, laws and moral codes, customs and calendar, history and traditions. In *Ice-Candy Man* a Brahmin Pandit loathes the very sight of a Muslim while taking his meal. 'He looks at his food as it is infected with maggots' and throws it away.

When Mountbatten told Jinnah that his demand was tantamount to the partition of Bengal and Punjab, Jinnah reluctantly agreed. 'I do not care how little you give me,' he said, 'so long as you give it to me completely'.

Mountbatten now embarked upon the task of convincing Congress leaders of the necessity of partition. In the beginning few people desired the country's dismemberment. Gandhi declared that India would be divided 'over my dead body.' Nehru, Azad, and Master Tara Singh were vehemently opposed to the creation of Pakistan. However, Mountbatten made use of two opposite lines of reasoning to prevail upon them. On the one hand, he declared that the truncated Pakistan, if conceded now, was bound to come back later. On the other hand, he promised that if India's two unwilling wings were lopped off, a strong and united centre would be the result. The second argument appealed to Sardar Patel who as Home Minister was already giving thought to the country's internal security. Moreover, he was vexed with the disruptionist tactics played by the Muslim League in the Interim

Government. Mountbatten overcame Nehru's objections by making an appeal to his democratic instincts. Now it was time to speak with Gandhi. In a last desperate effort, he suggested making Jinnah the head of government of an undivided India. The Muslim leader could select the entire ministry himself. But Patel and Nehru were unwilling to expose themselves to Jinnah's caprices. Even the League rejected the proposal calling it 'fantastic.' Finally, even Gandhi relented, feeling 'defeated and forsaken.' Thus Mountbatten played a very vital role in shaping the destiny of the nation. In the novel *Azadi*, it is shown that Mountbatten duped everyone into the division of the country and even Gandhi and Nehru failed to hold their balance before him. Then, he worked out a revised scheme thereby managing all the leaders to agree to partition.

Boundary Commissions were set up to delineate frontiers between Muslim and non-Muslim areas of Punjab and Bengal. 'It dealt out Indian cities,' in the words of Bapsi Sidhwa, 'like a pack of cards'. Chaman Nahal also brings out the fact that it was 'an impossible task' for Sir Cyril Radcliffe, Chairman of the Boundary Commission, 'to cut the country in two in five weeks' time especially when Indian judges on the commission were warring with each other on communal grounds. He had ignored their rival claims, and as impartially as he could divided the country."[17] Provinces which opted for Pakistan were North-West Frontier Province, West Punjab, Baluchistan and Sind. Later Mountbatten formally announced partition of the country to the effect of which India and Pakistan came into being.

Partition became a reality because the leaders had failed to manoeuvre 'politics as an exercise of negotiation, as the technique of neutralising tensions, as the way of creatively engaging with the aspirations of ordinary people, as the art of achieving what seems to be impossible' (Neera Chandhoke). Not only was the country split into two halves but also the Muslim community was divided into two nations; almost all the communities were hopelessly fragmented.

No one liked the vivisection of India, certainly not the way it came about. Pakistan along with the division of Indian Muslims into two nationalities was hardly the ideal that the

Muslim League was dreaming of. The man who had coined the term, Pakistan, Rahmat Ali, left Pakistan for England in frustration in 1948, authored *The Great Betrayal*, and died there. The Congress was unhappy at the division of India into two separate states; the League was disappointed at the division of Pakistan into two widely separated lands and of Indian Muslims into two Indian nationalities, India and Pakistan.

With the announcement of partition, people of India and Pakistan began to dread, to quote Chaman Nahal, the visitation of 'a prehistoric monster.' They woke up to find that a great tragedy accompanied freedom. They were deeply cut by the decision, for one reason or the other, to divide the country. To quote Azad:

> When partition had become a reality, even the Muslims who were the followers of the League were horrified by the result and started to say openly that this was not what they had meant partition.[18]

As it was, millions of Punjabis and Bengalis were uprooted from their ancestral homes and set wandering eastwards or westwards. How many thousands perished on the way 'will never be known.' The disaster had its explanations. India and Pakistan were at the moment of their birth like 'a pair of Siamese twins' linked by a cancerous tumour, Punjab. Cyril Radcliffe's scalpel had severed the tumour, but it had not been able to carve out the cancerous cells infecting each half.

The two nations, India and Pakistan, were engulfed by the most massive migration in human history. From one end of the Punjab to the other, a terrified people were fleeing their homes with whatever possessions they could carry. Across the border the militant communities prepared to drive their opponents from their midst so that they could gather on to the abandoned lands of their brothers whom Radcliffe's scalpel had left in Pakistan. In *Ice-Candy Men*, Bapsi Sidhwa paints the picture of a hoard of Sikh looters chasing the Muslims, and forcing them to leave their homes.

> They are like swarms of locusts, moving in marauding bands of thirty and forty thousand. They are killing all Muslims. Setting forces, looting, parading the Muslim women naked through the streets—raping and mutilating them in the centre of villages and in mosques.[19]

In *Azadi,* Nahal brings out the fact that 'many cities of the Punjab had been aflame for months'. He gives the extent of havoc in West Punjab wrought by the Muslims.

> The Hindu population had been completely driven out—or completely exterminated. Hindu and Sikh places of worship had obviously been defiled,... in one small village of twenty houses, every single house had been destroyed and there was not a soul in sight.[20]

However, in most instances people were stripped of, all their belongings before they were allowed to leave. They were rushing towards their promising lands of safety. They become, inevitably, the mongers of the terrible hysteria sweeping the Punjab. They spread the virus wherever they passed with their tales of woe, thereby, they created in turn new outbursts of violence. Death stalked across northern parts of the sub-continent. To quote Carry Collins and Dominique Lapierre:

> There would be no sanctuary from its scourge, no corner free from the contagion of its virus... It was not a war, not a civil war, not a guerrilla campaign. It was a convulsion, the sudden shattering collapse of the society.[21]

The plight of the minorities and of the refugees was beyond description. Nahal brings the whole picture before the reader's mind.

> Virtually the entire five hundred and fifty miles of the border between East and West Punjab was used by minorities to cross from one side to the other, the people heading for the point nearest to their own homes. Many starvation deaths in other convoys were reported, and it was common knowledge that only about half the number of any convoy got through safely. They perished of hunger, or disease, or exposure or they were killed by violence.[22]

The terrible anguish of those days in the Punjab meted out with almost biblical balance, an eye for an eye, massacre for massacre, rape for rape, blind cruelty for blind cruelty. It was like 'slow-motion images of a building disintegrating under the impact of an explosion, the walls of Punjab society crumbled upon each other.' "This is, as Iqbal Masood puts it, a mass psychosis. It is hopeless to fight against it."[23] Everyone seemed regressing. Only death and carnage seemed to be proceeding ahead. A terrible chapter of blood and tears was being added to history, a chapter without precedent.

A well-known writer and philanthropist, Khuda Baksh, observed in the beginning of the 20th century.

> In mutual help and co-operation lies our hope, in division and dissension our feebleness and death.[24]

The fears of the poet proved prophetic.

The ideologues of the Pakistan movement harped on the familiar theme of perpetual Hindu-Muslim conflicts, the strength of divisive forces and the contradictions between the 'Islamic' and 'Hindu' traditions. Their views based on the writings of Henry Elliot and other colonial writers who had reasons to project a distorted image of Indian society and its history. Admittedly, a fragmented form of religious consciousness had existed. But then integrative and syncretic forces were at work both at the elite and popular levels. Unfortunately, so far in human history, sectarianism is more prevalent, more insidious than mutual respect and tolerance. The results of this deep and widening divisions have been very disastrous when religion has mixed itself up with politics. In fact, there were many causes—religious, social, cultural and economic—which, strong enough, brought about alienation, among the major communities, Hindus, Muslims and Sikhs.

J.B. Priestly, in an essay entitled "Block Thinking', says that human beings belong to various blocks—racial, national, social, political, religious, etc., Their way of thinking and attitude and, in short, mindset, is coloured and conditioned by the block they align themselves with. They feel safe and secure and gain recognition by the outfit they wear. They get so inextricably entrenched in their respective blocks that they fail to appreciate the existence and validity of the other blocks. One such block of great magnitude is religion. It is a paradox that religion is at once a cohesive and divisive force. It has been argued that the two faiths—Hinduism and Islam—on the subcontinent are very different. The differences between them are palpable and striking. The British made it a point to keep them at daggers drawn. John Stratchay, an eminent civilian, has remarked:

> The existence of hostile creeds among the Indian people, side by side in one of the strong points of our political position in India.[25]

It is interesting to study how the paths diverged and differences cropped up among the followers of different faiths in question. With the advent of Islam a new world order began to make its impact on the subcontinent.

Islam is a religion with a founder, a revealed dogma and with a churchly establishment. It reposes faith in the prophet, and the Quran. "For the Hindu society, religion is a highly personal affair. There is no organised church, and shades of faith within the Hindu fold are more than ever the customary colours of the rainbow in the sky."[26] For Islam, the creator stands apart from His creation, ordering and presiding over His work. To the Hindu, the creator and his creation are one and indivisible. The Hindu, as a result, worships God in almost any form he chooses. A great European Indologist, Sir Charles Eliot, once wrote, "Hinduism has not been made, but has grown. It is a jungle, not a building. It is a living example of great national paganism such as might have existed in Europe if Christianity had not become the state religion of the Roman Empire, if there had remained an incongruous jumble of old superstitions and oriental cults." To the Muslim, on the contrary, there is but one God and the Quran forbids the faithful to represent him in any shape or form. Idols and idolatry to the Muslim, therefore, are abhorrent.

The greatest barrier in Hindu-Muslim understanding, however, is not religious but social. Muslims often claim that Pakistan came into being not only because Muslims in India were intensely conscious of their national and cultural identity, but also because the Hindu community in India was intolerant and exclusive. In any case, Hindus were much more stratified than any other community in India. So they employed religious rhetoric much more aggressively to compensate for lack of political unity in the community. Ambedkar has remarked that 'these castes are anti-national. They are anti-national because they bring about separation in social life.' Muslims argued that just as caste Hindus had maintained caste-segregation against Hindu inferior castes, the Hindu community dominated by Brahmins has also regarded Muslims, who ate beef and brought with them an alien culture as *malechas* (unclean) as shown in Cracking India when a Brahmin, on seeing yours at expressed 'a terror, passion and pain expected of a violated virgin' because he could not bear the sight of an outcast, an untouchable excrescence.'

Further to save themselves from the process of Islamisation the Hindus tightened their social structure, which was already rigid and had little room for flexibility. The caste-ridden social structure of the Hindus was anathema for the Muslims. Thus despite close association for centuries the Hindus and the Muslims remained two distinct communities among whom inter-dining and inter-marriage were prohibited. As long as Muslims were the rulers, they did not mind their social alienation from the Hindus. But once they ceased to be rulers, their sense of alienation from the mass of Hindu society became a cause of concern and fear.

Hindus and Muslims received education from their denominational schools. In Punjab, for instance, Hindu children acquired few scraps of knowledge from the village pandit who taught them in Punjabi. But Muslim children would get their education from a sheikt, in the mosque reciting Quran in a different language, Urdu. Even the primitive drugs and potions they used were based on different systems of natural medicine—Unani and Ayurveda.

Another thing which always keeps the two communities at loggerheads is music and the cow. Music never accompanies the austere service of the mosque and its strains mingled with 'the mumble of their prayers' is blasphemous. There was no surer way for the Hindus to incite their Muslim neighbours than to set up a band outside a mosque during Friday prayers. In *Tamas*, people in the city were all agog, watching 'with bated breath' when a procession playing music was taking place because it would result in riots. For the Muslim the favourite provocation involved is an animal, the sacred cow. The thought of worshipping a dumb animal was repugnant to the Muslims. They would take a perverse delight in driving a lowing, protesting herd of cows to the slaughter house.

To those social and religious differences had been added an even more divisive, more insidious distinction, economic. The Hindus had been far swifter than the Muslims in seizing the opportunities. British education and western thought had opened up a wide world of employment. The Muslims and the Hindus competed against each other not only for government posts but also for jobs and opportunities created in the wake of industrialisation and urbanisation in India. As the Muslims lagged behind in education, they could not vie with the Hindus. So the Muslim middle-class, starting from a backward position in this competitive struggle 'found the idea of Pakistan extremely attractive' because that would mean Muslim banks, Muslim industries, and Muslim commercial houses established in Muslim Pakistan with the fear of Hindu competition removed permanently from their state. It is significant to note that Muslim commercial communities like Memons and the Khojas in Bombay and Calcutta gave considerable financial support to the Muslim League particularly during the elections of 1945-46. It may also be noted that Jinnah who was a Khoja by origin and a successful lawyer in Bombay, enjoyed the support from the commercial communities more than any other Muslim leader, and this gave him a distinct advantage over leaders from the other areas like Punjab and Bengal. In the urban areas, the Hindus were the dominant community. The ubiquitous role of the moneylender was almost everywhere discharged by Hindus partly because of the Quranic proscription preventing

Muslims from practising usury. The Muslim upper classes, many of whom descended from the Moghul invaders, had tended to remain landlords and soldiers. The Muslim masses were usually landless peasants or workers in the service of Hindu employees in the city. The economic rivalry accentuated the social and religious barriers between the two communities. The imbalance between the relative positions of the Hindus and the Muslims created the first stirrings of communal consciousness which was largely the product of reactionary thinking and British tactics. But it played upon the fears which naturally came to a minority. They began to take an increasingly sectarian stance and the result, naturally enough, was an increase in communal consciousness which in turn resulted in partition.

Partition, as reservoir of a great national experience, should have found creative expression. Yet, curiously enough, this tragic and momentous event has not stirred the creative imagination and urge of many Indian-English writers. Only a few novelists have treated it seriously and what is more surprising is that none of the foremost novelists—Mulk Raj Anand, R.K. Narayan and Raja Rao, for instance,—has concentrated upon it in any one of their novels except as passing remarks. Bhabani Bhattacharya is fully aware of this fact, and regrets that a fairly good number of novelists have not felt a strong creative urge to recreate this event. In contrast, the two world wars are adequately reflected in the best literature of the West. The writers have lived through history undazed. The major older novelists' indifference to the partition is not wholly inexplicable. They did not chance to see and feel the actualities of the trauma.

However, the observations, made above, do not imply that the theme of partition has not been explored in Indian English fiction. It has been a compelling experience, resulting in irresistible creative urge, for several Indian-English novelists. Novelists like Khushwant Singh, Manohar Malgonkar, Raj Gill, Chaman Nahal, Bhisham Sahi, Bapsi Sidhwa, Shauna Singh stand out prominently among those who have treated the theme of partition, in detail. R.K. Narayan, Balachandra Rajan, Attia Hosain and others have dealt with it cursorily as a side issue in their novels.

This study makes an attempt to study the theme of partition in Khushwant Singh's *Train to Pakistan*, Chaman Nahal's *Azadi* and Bhisham Sahni's *Tamas* which present the Indian perception of the traumatic experiences and Bapsi Sidhwa's *Ice-Candy Man* which projects the Pakistani version, though both the versions are free from religious bias and do not follow other sectarian lines.

REFERENCES

1. Maulana Abdul Kalam Azad: *India Wins Freedom* (New Delhi: Orient Longman Ltd., 1988) p. 201.
2. Peter Heehs: *India's Freedom Struggle* (Delhi: Oxford University Press, 1988) p. 152.
3. Aziz Ahmed: *'Islamic National Movement,'* Ed. by A.L. Basham (Delhi: Oxford University Press, 1975) p. 385.
4. Peter Heehs: *India's Freedom Struggle,* p. 155.
5. Sahni Bhisham: *Tamas* (New Delhi: Penguin Books, 1988) p. 32.
6. Bipin Chandra: *Communalism in Modern India* (New Delhi: Vikas Publishing Pvt. Ltd., 1987) p. 159.
7. Mushirul Hasan: *Nationalism and Communal Politics in India* (New Delhi: Manohar Publishing, 1991) p. 25.
8. Patel Bhaichand: "Hindu Revivalists are Mimicking Islamic Fundamentalists: Khushwant Singh and V.S. Naipal in Conversation," *Outlook*, May 8, 2000, p. 59.
9. Sahni Bhisham: *Tamas,* p. 168.
10. Bipin Chandra: *Communism in Modern India,* p. 159.
11. Peter Heehs: *Indian Freedom Struggle*, p. 158.
12. Percial Spear: *History of India*, Volume II (Penguin Eleventh Impression, 1998), p. 278.
13. Bipin Chandra: *Communalism in Modern India*, p. 143.
14. Peter Heehs: *India's Freedom Struggle*, p. 162.
15. Tara Chand: *History of Modern India* (New Delhi: Publication Division, Ministry of Information and Broadcasting, Government of India, 1974), p. 488.
16. Tara Chand: *History of Modern India,* p. 372.
17. Nahal Chaman: *Azadi*, p. 214.
18. Abdul Kalam Azad: *India Wins Freedom* (New Delhi: Orient Longman Ltd., 1988), p. 224.

19. Bapsi Sidhwa: *Ice-Candy Man*, p. 197.
20. Nahal Chaman: *Azadi.*, p. 283.
21. Mishirul Hasan: *Nationalism and Communal Politics in India* (Delhi: Manohar Publications, 1994), p. 175.
22. Nahal Chaman: *Azadi*, p. 257.
23. Iqbal Masood: *Dream Merchants, Politicians and Partition* (Delhi: HarperCollins Publishers Ltd., 1997), p. 13.
24. Larry Collins and Dominique Lapierre: *Freedom at Midnight* (New Delhi: Vikas Publishing Housing Pvt. Ltd., 1975), p. 284.
25. B.C. Grover and S. Graves: *A New Look at Modern Indian History* (New Delhi: S. Chand and Company Ltd., 1998), p. 2411.
26. N.K. Sinha: *Islam in India* (Patna: Oriental Public Library, 1996), p. 176.

Train to Pakistan

Khushwant Singh was born in 1915 in a village called Sargoda, which is now in Pakistan. He studied in Delhi and Lahore and then moved to King's College, London. Later he practised at Lahore High Court before joining the Indian Ministry of External Affairs in 1947. With 64 books to his credit, Khushwant Singh dons well the triple roles, as a short story-writer, novelist and religious historian. As a religious historian his most enduring work has been done in the field of Sikh history and biography. His brilliant portrait of Ranjit Singh vividly brings out the leader, the ruler and the man. He has published a few novels, *Train to Pakistan, I Shall Not Hear the Nightingale, Delhi, The Company of Women* and two collections of short stories, *The Mark of Vishnu* and *A Bride for the Sahib.*

There are three kinds of environments which influenced Khushwant Singh as man and writer. He was born and brought up in childhood in a Punjabi village: 'My roots are in the dunghill of a tiny Indian village.' Then he went to school in Lahore and Delhi where he lives: 'I grew up in Indo-Anglian atmosphere of New Delhi.' Later he went abroad for higher education. He is what the British education made him, a cultured humanist. 'I am the product of both the East and the West. I am, if I may coin the word, an Orio-occidental.' All these influences can be traced in his works.

Train to Pakistan is the touching tale of a village, Mano Majra, struck down by the hate and the violence that came with the division of the sub-continent when a train-load of massacred men, women and children arrive in the village. It reveals with pitiless precision a picture of the bestial horrors enacted on the Indo-Pakistan border during the days of 1947. The predominant features of the novel are its stark realism, its absolute fidelity to the truth and, above all, its trenchant exposure of the partition-horrors. Mano Majra, a remote village in the North-Western region of undivided India, serves as the fictional setting of the novel. Although traditionally devoid of political consciousness, the village emerges as a microcosm of India. As Hindus and Sikhs battled their Muslim 'brothers' for a political stronghold in the newly-liberated nation, India, the villagers' traditional ways of life progressively disintegrated into selfishness, mistrust, and cruelty. Lala Ram Lal, a Hindu moneylender, was murdered by a dacoit, Malli, but the police bungled the case in such a way that the Sikhs of the village began to look askance at the Muslims. The villagers were carried away when they saw people from either side of the boundary on their way, seeking refuge and security. Most of the Sikhs were all rage when they had come to know that their Sikh brethren had been subjected to heinous cruelties by the Muslims in Pakistan. The Muslims in the village were dazed at the predatory advances of the Sikhs in the surrounding villages and resolved to leave for Pakistan, the land of Islamic faith and promise. But the Sikhs were unrelented and would not like to leave the Muslims unscathed. They stretched a wire rope across the bridge in order to kill the people sitting on the roof of the train. However, Jugga, a Sikh, slashed at the rope whereby he sets an example of supreme sacrifice. He puts an end to his life for the sake of enabling the Muslims, particularly his beloved, Nooran, to reach Pakistan safely. The love story is used to the exigencies of the political upheaval, which along with the conflicting motives of the leaders at the helm of affairs, are not dealt with comprehensively as Nahal does in *Azadi*.

How harmony degenerates into disharmony is traced with humanistic concern. Khushwant Singh projects Mano Majrans as bright and breezy, contented and calm during the tumultuous times while most of the other villages in the country were reeling under the burden of communalism. In their happy ignorance of ghastly riots the Muslims and Sikhs of this village still clung to the ideals preached by Gandhi, even though Gandhi himself was then "walking the bloody paths of the riot-torn India of his dream, lonely and disillusioned."[1] Nevertheless, Mano Majra seems to be typical where people belonging to various religions lived in amity. Sikhs and Muslims, more or less, were equally distributed in the village. Lala Ram Lal was the only Hindu family. Surprisingly all the villagers venerated three-foot slab of sandstone, Deo, the local deity, "all the villagers—Hindu, Sikh and Muslim or pseudo-Christian—repair secretly whenever they are in special need of blessing."[2] Imam Bakh and Meet Singh, the religious heads of the Muslims and Sikhs, respectively, waited for each other to 'make the first call.' The Muslim Mullah, Imam Baksh endeared himself to the villagers as '*chacha* or uncle.' 'Bhai' Meet Singh was one of the many who did not have any grouses on the basis of religion. He represented the tension-free life of the Mano Majrans when he said to the social worker, Iqbal:

> Everyone is welcome to his religion. Here next door is a Muslim mosque. When I pray to my Guru, uncle Imam Baksh calls to Allah...(p. 35)

To quote K.R. Srinivasa Iyengar, "Here's functional "integration", and indeed there are tens of thousands of villages like Mano Majra, where the law has always been peaceful co-existence, and not communal strife."[3] With the arrival of the ghost-train the age-old harmony between the communities was shattered but the Sikhs of the village did not nourish any ill-will though communal passions had been in the air.

Khushwant Singh shows when things go pell-mell, even the majority will be afflicted with fear complex which is further accentuated by a faulty reading of history. When things are misrepresented the consequences are ghastly and reason and logic are put behind. It started with the murder of Lala Ram Lal by a Malli, a dacoit. The murder was interpreted in such a way that in no time it gained communal overtones. The police enquiry had sown the seeds of mistrust among the Muslims and the Hindus. The doubts of the police about the Mano Majrans and the whereabouts of Sultana and Iqbal made the Sikhs look at Muslim community with an air of suspicion. In fact the visit of the police "had divided Mano Majra into two halves as neatly as a knife cuts through a pat of butter" (p. 105). The whole Sikh community sank into silence and everyone began to feel his neighbours' hand against him, and was anxious to distinguish friends from foes. The recollection of the faint smell of searing flesh which they had smelt when corpses from the ghost train had been burnt a few days ago, sent 'a chill down their spine.'

> Quite suddenly every Sikh in Mano Majra becomes a stranger with an evil intent. His long hair and beard appear barbarous, his kirpan menacingly anti-Muslim. (p. 105)

Similarly, a sense of fear, the fear of suppression and domination by the Muslims, gripped the Sikhs' minds. As they remembered what their Gurus had exhorted them— 'never trust a Muslim'—they became 'sullen and angry.' Iqbal's reported aim to spy on them was another shock and this jolted them out of the cocoon of complacency and well-being.

> We have looked upon the Muslims as our brothers and sisters. Why should they send somebody to spy on us? (p. 105)

The seeds of suspicion, thus taken root, spread rapidly as both the communities adopted diametrically opposite and hostile position with their faulty understanding of history for which the British were mainly responsible. "Many of the British historians were often guided by broad considerations other than those of historical survey. First, they wanted to see the fact that the Indian people had always been ruled by cruel tyrants and uncontrolled despots."[4] The British education propagated these vicious ideas which, without given to any reflection, were imbibed and propagated by the Indians. The Sikhs in Mano Majra called up the atrocities inflicted upon their forefathers by the barbaric and cruel Muslims. History taught them how they and the Hindus had been put to innumerable insults by the Muslims and how time and again their children and women were tortured.

> All through the Muslim period of Indian history...what had they done to Sikhs?...hundreds of thousands had been put to the sword for no other offence than refusing to accept Islam; their temples had been desecrated by the slaughter of kine; the holy Grandh torn to bits. (p. 106)

Thus the British historian stressed the point that the Muslims and others had waged wars only on religious grounds. "The myth of Muslim rapine and destruction was thus utilized in order to stress the point that there was nothing wrong if the British rule too was autocratic and despotic. But what makes the difference was that their (the British) rule was benevolent and just and operated under the rule of law."[5] This sort of interpretation of historical facts gives communal overtones and even the arrest of Iqbal and the murder of Ram Lal, sparked off fears in both the communities. The Britishers, thus encouraged as many divisions as they could resulted in communal carnage. Iyengar says, "There is enough evidence to convict the British administrators who after a hundred years of trusteeship could only prepare for this holocaust."[6] But then Indians could not evade the responsibility of keeping themselves united, rising above sectarian and communal thoughts. In an interview to Amitava Kumar, Khushwant Singh has observed: "When we got independence we were all under the illusion that the communal divide is now over once and for all. It was the British who had encouraged it. They were gone and there would be no more communal tension in the country. That proved to be wrong. We have had more communal violence since independence. Hindu-Muslim riots and even Hindu-Sikh riots and Hindu-Christian violence have gone to an almost nauseating extent. If people have some kind of prejudice or hate in their hearts, it does come out."

The aura of mistrust, suspicion, fear and false reading of history caused religiosity. Making use of one's religion to non-spiritual issues with a view to promoting the interests of a community proved to be very detrimental in the long run. The Sikh youth, for instance, mediating to avenge on behalf of his Sikh brethren, chanted the verse.

> By the grace of God
>
> Will bear the world nothing but goodwill (p. 132)

When religious fervour gets hold of an individual, he would run riot. In any case, communalism involved none of the people's real-life demands or interests. The fear complex could be fully aroused by propagating that their religious interests and their religion itself were in danger. The Sikhs were all agog that their religion would be at stake owing to the possible onslaught of the Muslims. He recalled:

> What had they done to Sikhs? Executed two of their Gurus, assassinated another and butchered his infant children; hundreds of thousands had been put to the sword for no other offence than refusing to accept Islam. (p. 106)

In fact, some such emotionalising and inflammable factor is needed to raise communal politics to the level of popular movement. Even the educated could not help succumbing to communal passions. The 'city-bred militant youths' who symbolise false religiosity fumed and fretted that the Sikhs had sent the Muslims alive. The unenlightened peasantry belonging to Sikhs was soon instigated by the educated. The leader of the group asked them to take revenge constantly harping on the words 'Hindu', 'Sikh' and 'Muslim' in order to work them into furies.

> ...for each Hindu or Sikh they kill, kill two Mussulmans. For each woman they abduct or rape, abduct two... (p. 129)

The villagers could not withstand this line of argument. Their reason was clouded and they ran amuck. Even the news that the Muslim brethren of their village had already evacuated and would depart for Pakistan could not stop them from the execution of the plot. In this context what Khalid has observed is worthwhile: 'Perhaps a dominant and decisive cause of Pakistan is that there has never taken a confluence of the two civilizations in India—the Hindu and the Muslim. They may have meandered towards each other here and there, but on the whole, the two have flowed their separate courses—sometimes parallel and sometimes contraryto one another.

Ethics, which should be 'the kernel of a religious code,' has been carefully removed. Iqbal, a better philosopher than social worker, found religion hollow and devoid of values. He believed that India 'devoid of religious faith had been constipated a lot of humbug.' He contemplated:

> Take religion. For the Hindu, it means little besides caste and cow protection. For the Muslim, circumcision and Kosher meat. For the Sikh, long hair and hatred of the Muslim. For the Christian, Hinduism with a sola topee. For the Parsee, fire-worship and feeding vultures. (p. 149)

Religion, with 'the soulless world', could only be the cause of barriers creating disharmony and discord as in the case of the Indians. In crucial moments they could not shape and define their existence through thought and decision but succumbed to emotion and failed miserably.

Partition is, it has been argued, the result of the failure of 'Gandhi-caps,' those leaders preaching non-violence. But Khushwant Singh seems uninterested to delve deep into the motives of the leaders, who were, in one way or the other way round, accountable for the division and the mass hysteria that followed it. Nevertheless, the writer appears to give vent to his feelings in the case of Jawaharlal Nehru, who failed to act and to rise to the occasion.

> ...where was the power?...Long ago we made a tryst with destiny and now the time comes when we shall redeem our pledge not wholly or in the fully measure but very substantially. Yes, Mr. Prime Minister, you made your tryst. So did many others on the 15th August, Independence Day. (p. 122)

Perhaps it is not correct to blame Nehru squarely for what happened during the days of partition. It may be plausible to argue that 'the prince of Hamlet,' Nehru, could not rise to the occasion. Like other leaders, he too was stunned by the magnitude of the carnage and the communal cruelty of which his people had suddenly shown themselves capable was a shocking revelation to him. He was said to be "physically ill at the stark, direct confrontation with the miseries overwhelming so many of his countrymen."[7]

The novelist captures well the nuances of the feelings and the emotional response of the Muslims when they were rather compelled to leave their homes for good. The rural population of Punjab were not at all prepared for the big holocaust which the partition proved to be and "it came as a big destablising factor in the smug and contented self-sufficiency of the Indian rural life."[8] They were caught in a disaster beyond their understanding. They sat and moped in their houses. They had heard of the atrocities committed by Sikhs on Muslims and of "mosques being desecrated by the slaughter of the pigs on the premises and of copies of the holy Koran being torn up" (p. 103). They came to know that the Muslims from other villages had been evacuated to the refugee camps and arrangements had been made for their crossing the border. With heavy hearts, they decided to go away. However, the decision created scenes of gloom and pangs of separation. Imam Baksh broke into tears observing: "What have we to do with Pakistan? We were born here. So were our ancestors. We have lived amongst you as your brothers" (p. 110). It was extremely shocking to go away from what they knew to be their home. The women sat on the floors hugging each other and crying. It was as if in every home there had been a death. They were assured of all help and protection by the Sikhs of the village. But the irate refugees pouring in from Pakistan posed a threat. Hence they were advised to go to the refugee camp for a few days.

Khushwant Singh is very critical when he unfolds Iqbal, a replica of a cunning political leader in the garb of socialism who came to Mano Majra not to stem in communal carnage and make sacrifice but to watch the drama at the village as it was 'a vital point for refugee movements.' His mission was to keep the village unaffected by communalism. But his sarcasm and nihilistic approach dampened the spirit of everyone. He made a mockery of the nation's problem as an off-shoot of the high annual birth rate. Towards the conclusion, he came to know that no corner was free from 'the contagion of communal virus.' When he was informed that the train, heading for Pakistan with Muslim refugees from Mano Majra would be attacked, in a fit of emotion, he thought of sacrificing himself in an attempt to avert the tragedy. But he found sacrifice futile if there was none to see and admire the supreme act. The aspiring reformer had a proclivity to interpret every situation in terms of violence for the sake of obtaining political and economic stability. In sharp satiric relief, however, the author portrays Iqbal as an aristocratic imposter, a snob and a fraud.

Khushwant Singh seems to suggest that life is purposeful because it produces men like Bhai Meet Singh who rejected religious bigotry and opted for humanism. He did not see any reason why the Muslims be punished for the crimes their fellow brothers were committing in Pakistan. He felt that the guilty should be punished. There was 'awed silence' when Meet Singh said: "What have the Muslims here done to us for us to kill them in revenge for what Muslims in Pakistan are doing? But it was the savage law, an eye for an eye, a tooth for a tooth, which had carried away the people's emotion. The priest's voice was too weak to be heard in the hubbub of the communal frenzy. But then, as Srinivasa Iyengar says: It is the still small voice of sanity, the voice of reason, the voice of humanity."[9]

Khushwant Singh shows, without much sentimentality, the triumph of love, of humanism, of faith in the goodness of man in a moment of real crisis and challenge which is, perhaps, the focal point of the novel. The rough Jugga— 'a self-confessed *budmash*'—after his release, came to know the attack on the train must mean danger to his Nooran, a Muslim girl. He made up his mind to prevent the attack, if necessary at the risk of his own life. According to the plan of the avengers, a rope 'stiff as a shaft of steel' was tied across the first span of the bridge to finish off the passengers boarded on the train. With his kirpan, he slashed at the rope that was designed to bring about the train disaster. 'There is a volley of shots. The man shivers and collapses.' The rope snapped in the centre as he fell. 'The train went over him, and went on to Pakistan' with all the Muslim refugees. Thus the supreme sacrifice came from the most unexpected quarter. At a time when the bureaucracy, the intelligentsia, the men of religion and the political leadership failed to act, Jugga proved his mettle. Whatever be the motivation for his action, the fact remains that he did the incredible. It may be, as Srinivasa Iyengar puts it, 'a speck in the dust-whirl that was the partition.' The passion of one man saved hundreds of innocent people. To quote Chirantan Kulshrestha:

> Jugga's act of love and sacrifice silhouetted against the backdrop of hatred and violence, towers above the communal differences and lends a meaning to the general aimlessness of life in the partition days.[10]

Jugga is a man of action, a man who is not lost in the jungle of ideologies, nor lost in the labyrinthine thought processes. He is essentially a man whose actions contribute harmony and integration. 'When there is no disintegration, no conflict, no struggle to become, only then there is the being of the whole, the complete (J. Krishna Murthy).

When asked in what way *A Train to Pakistan* is different from the other Indian writing, Khushwant Singh replies: "Perhaps it was the first novel on the partition theme and totally unbiased."[11] The novelist blames squarely on all the communities entrenched deeply in the violent upheaval. He pulls the people involved to pieces for their active participation in instigating the masses to mutiny and killing. He exposes, without any reservations, how the "Mullas roamed Punjab and the Frontier Province with boxes of human skull said to be those of Muslims in Bihar with an intention to work up Muslims (p. 94). Again, Jugga described the barbarity of Buluch soldiers on their way to Lahore from Amritsar. Reaching near the Pakistani border, these soldiers 'began to stick bayonets into Sikhs along the road.'

Perhaps to balance the heinous acts perpetrated by the Muslims to the Sikhs, he narrated the story of the four Sikh Sardars, who went on rampage riding in a jeep alongside, a mile-long column of Muslim refugees, trekking laboriously.

> ...without warning they opened fire with their sten guns. Four sten guns! God alone knows how many they killed... (p. 61)

He shows very clearly that the Sikhs grew rash quickly and 'logic was never a strong point with Sikhs.' He rails against all those 'Hindu, Muslim, Sikh, Congressite, Leaguer, Akali, or Communist,' the sub-human species, who being 'deep in it'—were all out to slaughter some of their own kind. It is beyond doubt that the novel is refreshingly free from communal bias.

Train to Pakistan presents the Indian perception of the traumatic experience which is free from religious bias. Khushwant Singh himself states: "I think it is a documentary novel of the partition, an extremely tragic event which hurt me very much. I had no animosity against either the Muslims or the Pakistanis, but I felt that I should do something to express that point of view."[12] Though he was not a sufferer of the riots, he knows the miseries that partition had unleashed.

Detachment in time helps the novelist because the greater the distance in time from the event, the less the likelihood of his remembering the details of the cataclysm subjectively. Singh wrote the novel after a lapse of more than a decade which would help him maintain aesthetic distance which gives him creative vision that transcends sectarianism and remains essentially human. His point of view does not follow narrow religious lines.

Since the novel deals with the theme of partition which is very expansive, the writer should be on his guard in evolving a suitable technique lest his realism degenerates into mere 'historical documentary.' So the technique he adopts should be such as to capture the spectrum of the cataclysmic events. Khushwant Singh's realistic portrayal seems to be successful since his art is revealed not merely in the profound probing into the real, but also in the transformation of the actual into symbols and images. The long rainless summer symbolises heavenly retribution for the communal riots. The weather, scorching sun and swelling rivers stand for the violence escalating beyond comprehension. The train is also a powerful symbol. Mono Majra was guided by the trains and it was when the ghost train passed through the village that the quiet and harmonious life came to a halt. Geckos and moths, too, enhance the effect of the looming tragedy. Two geckos fighting on the ceiling, a pervasive symbol of the novel, externalizes Hukum Chand's subjective state. The moth snatched up by the geckos is an image of everyone's destiny. The use of technique of contrast makes the novel very impressive. It highlights Jugga's noble intentions emanating from unfathomable love. Also, there is a vein of pungent irony in the novel. The Sikh militant planning to wreak vengeance on the Muslims chanted the verse from the scriptures.

> By the grace of God
>
> We bear the world nothing but good will (p. 132)

However, Jugga's sacrifice got religious sanction. Bhai Meet Singh, the priest, read out lines from the holy book when Jugga had gone over to seek Guru's blessings for his sacrifice. Writing on Khushwant Singh's art and technique, V.A. Shahane says:

> Khushwant Singh's art and technique of fiction show several notable features: his use of rhythm, especially of the train; his sensitive depiction of atmosphere,...his excellent portrayal of characters, 'round' rather than 'flat,' the exploration of their human context; his natural and almost effortless presentation of point of view through situation and character designed to convey the final significance of the novel.[13]

Khushwant Singh has succeeded, through resolved limitation and rigorous selection, in communicating to his readers a hint of the grossness, ghastliness of the partition-tragedy.

As the very first novelist on partition, Khushwant Singh is successful in that he portrays the harsh facts of life against the background of India's partition, its skilful dissection of the real. The compelling story of people in turmoil is far broader in its implications than its length might suggest. This is not the story of one man, Jugga, but the tale of a village "led to a moral action through its own indifference."[14] The directness, the simplicity and the compelling quality of Singh's narrative mode are all, perhaps, beyond critical enquiry. The novelist seems to deprecate the part played by the educated people of the country in causing devastation, making an irony of the whole movement of freedom. However, he does not offer penetrating insights into the causes of partition and the reasons for the sudden blindness with which the leaders were afflicted during those fateful days. Nevertheless, the novel appears unparalleled in its objective and realistic treatment of partition. Violence when viewed in retrospect often leads to descriptions that are simplistic or schematic. One of the triumphs of Khushwant Singh's writing in the novel, perhaps, is the way in which *Train to Pakistan* eludes such schematism.

REFERENCES

1. Govinda Prasad Sarma: *Nationalism in Indo-Anglian Fiction* (New Delhi: Sterling Publishers Limited, 1977-1978), p. 247.
2. Khushwant Singh: *Train to Pakistan* (Bombay: India Book House Pvt. Ltd., 1975), p. 2. Further reference to this text in this chapter will be cited parenthetically by page number.
3. K.R. Srinivasa Iyengar: *Indian Writing in English* (New Delhi: Sterling Publishers Pvt. Ltd., 1985), p. 498.
4. Bipin Chandra: *Communalism in Modern India*, p. 254.
5. *Ibid.*, p. 246.
6. K.R. Srinivasa Iyengar: *Indian Writing in English*, p. 501.
7. Larry Collins and Dominique Lapierre: *Freedom at Midnight*, p. 303.
8. R.K. Dhawan: *Three Contemporary Novelists* (New Delhi: Classical Publishing, 1985), p. 78.
9. K.R. Srinivasa Iyengar: *Indian Writing in English*, p. 500.
10. Meenakshi Mukherjee, ed.: *Considerations: Khushwant Singh's Fiction* by Chirantan Kulshrestha (New Delhi: Allied Publishers Pvt. Ltd., 1977) p. 152.
11. Interview with Khushwant Singh: Atma Ram *The Quest,* Vol. 7, October 1993, p. 72.
12. V.A. Shahane: *Khushwant Singh: An Artist in Realism,* ed. M.K. Naik, *Critical Essays on Indian Writing in English* (Delhi: Macmillan, 1977), p. 352.
13. V.A. Shahane: *Khushwant Singh: An Artist in Realism*, ed. M.K. Naik *Critical Essays on Indian Writing in English* (Delhi: Macmillan, 1977), p. 350.
14. Govinda Prasad Sarma: *Nationalism in Indo-Anglian Fiction* (New Delhi: Sterling Publishers, 1994), p. 77.

Azadi

Of the novelists of seventies, Chaman Nahal perhaps has shown vitality, variety, humanity and artistic integrity. His collection of short stories, *The Weird Dance* which came out in 1965, carved a niche for himself and placed him among the masters of Indian-English fiction. However, the real promise in creative writing is held out by his four novels—*My True Faces* (1973), *Azadi* (1975), *Into Another Dawn* (1977) and *English Queens* (1979). His forte seems to be writing historical fiction dealing with Gandhian era as evidenced in the quartet of which *Azadi* forms the last part. His achievement in the realm of fiction has been recognised by the conferment of the Sahitya Academy Award for his *Azadi*.

Born in Sialkot, Nahal was driven away to India after partition. He seizes upon the material from the traumatic experience and the result is *Azadi*. It was while writing *Azadi* that he became aware of the potentiality of an historical novel. In the novel he used history as a metaphor. He contemplated:

> ...couldn't he use the past to illustrate a theme that might have in mind. The artists have always leaned on myth for support.[1]

Nahal defines himself as 'essentially affirmationist' and a 'preserver of human values.' His claim to have captured 'the very rhythm of Indian life' sounds legitimate.

Chaman Nahal's *Azadi* enacts the hopeful dawn of Indian independence and the tragedy of partition—the massacres and the vast influx of refugees. Spanning from the announcement of the Cabinet Mission Plan on June 3, 1947 to the 'aftermath,' the murder of Gandhi, the novel is divided into three parts—The Lull, The Storm and The Aftermath. The significance of the titles is explicit.

Lala Kanshi Ram, an inhabitant of Sialkot, was leading a very contented life. Though partition was at hand, he along with the other minorities, Hindus and Sikhs, was lulled into a false sense of security, underwent tribulations and turmoils when they were uprooted from their homes. They went through a living inferno during their painful odyssey to India. Though they rode out of the storm, the agony continued unabated in the aftermath of their reaching the land of promise, India. Communal politics changed the very pattern of their lives, robbing them of the spirit out of their lives. Perhaps this is the novel to show how partition wrought havoc in the lives of a few individuals and highlight their psychological gyrations.

In the very beginning of the novel, it has been shown how communal leaders used different frame of references to incite one community against the other. The Hindu leaders, though they were a minor segment in the West Punjab, were inclined to whip up communal passions. The Hindu communal view was made to seep into the minds of people living in Punjab. This view states that Indian society and culture reached ideal heights in the ancient period. However, it fell into "continuous decay during the medieval period because of Muslim rule."[2] Consequently the ancient period was held to be sacrosanct and above critical study. No criticism of the ancient period was tolerated lest it should dilute the communal critique of the medieval period. In Sialkot, the Hindu communalists, under the auspices of Arya Samaj, defended the glory and grandeur of their religion to counter the majority community, the Muslims in Punjab and to repel their cultural onslaughts. As a member of Arya Samaj, Kanshi Ram was taught in no uncertain terms that 'the true heritage of an Indian was the Vedic.' In the clutches of the Samaj, he asserted:

No other nation in the world would never touch the glory of the Vedic civilization.[3]

Thus, Arya Samaj consciously promoted religiosity and orthodoxy as part of revival in Hinduism. This revivalism expressed in several different ways though its main core and contours were defined by "cow protection agitation, the crusade for Hindi, and the Sangathan of a caste-ridden society.'[4] It was in the meetings of the Samaj that Kanshi Ram came to know that the true language of an Indian was Sanskrit, the language of the Vedas. As he could not get that far back he was asked to learn Hindi, the modern derivative of Sanskrit. When the census was taken by the government he 'dutifully entered against the column for the mother tongue, the word Hindi'. The paradox is that 'he neither spoke Hindi nor ever wrote it on paper. Religiously or politically one identifies oneself with some group through tradition or habit, through impulse, prejudice, imitation or laziness. This identification puts an end to all creative understanding. Identification is in essence a thought process by which the mind safeguards and expands itself; and in becoming something it must resist and defend, it must own and discard. Then one becomes a mere tool in the hands of the party boss, the priest, or the favoured leader.

Arya Samaj's crusade for Hindi drew the lines of cleavage between the Hindus and the Muslims in Punjab. The Muslims suspected some foul play because the Hindus under the banner of the Samaj clamoured that Urdu should be replaced by Hindi as it was conceived to be the language of Muslims.

In their instigation of the common people, in particular and in their communal propaganda the Muslim communalists did not lag behind. Their control over the Muslim masses of lower middle class was unquestioned and complete as was shown in the case of Abdul Ghani. The leaguers successfully made him 'aware of the threat in a free India.' It was with little difficulty that they made forays into his thought pattern because unlettered as he was he could not act on his own and, moreover, he was very gullible like many of the poor belonging to the Muslim masses easily carried away by the oratory of their leaders. He himself conceded the fact, reflecting in a characteristic vein of an ignoramus.

> It was not a question of his personal view; the League or Jinnah knew better. They said, view you Hindu neighbour with suspicion and he did that. They said there should be a Pakistan, and he shouted for it. (p. 56)

Having been trained up in this fashion, he became so 'impudent' and haughty that he called Kanshi Ram, 'Kanshi Rama.' Kanshi Rama appeared to him a replica of a Hindu bania, a Shylock as concocted by the League. This way of educating people proved to be very detrimental to the unity and integrity of the nation in the making.

With the spread of education communalism branched out in a number of ways. The setting up of denominational schools was one of its ramifications. Though children were little affected in their tender years, the schools would definitely be insidious catalysts, promoting communal interests to a large extent. A large number of Congress and Muslim League leaders imbibed some of the elements and propagated them freely. In Sialkot, there were 'government school, Arya Samaj school, then Islamia and at the other end Khalsa. The schools of this sort would organise a communal, distorted and unscientific view of history, thereby whipping up communal passions. They had been set up with a clear intention to foster their vested interests and to denounce the other communities whose avowed aim, according to them, was to prey upon them. In this context what Lala Lajpat Rai, a Punjabi Congress leader, said in his autobiography about a similar context is worth-noting:

> At that time a book on Indian history called *Waquiat-i-Hind* used to be taught at government schools. The book created in me the feeling that Mussalmans had subjected the Hindus to great tyranny. Gradually the respect for Islam that I had acquired from my early training began to change into hatred because of *Waquiat-i-Hind*.[5]

Nehru's comment on the subject is revealing. He says that the history and economics and other subjects were taught in the schools and colleges written 'entirely from the British view-point, and laid stress on our numerous failings in the past and present and the virtues and the high destiny of the British.'

There could not be any intellectual escape from it for they knew no other facts. It may be conjectured that these schools in Sialkot were clear signs of different communities going their separate ways. When one school outstripped another in 'academic distinctions,' in sports or in debates the boys worked themselves into furies in the streets. "Heads were broken and later communal shape was given to these fights" (p. 99). Thus the very philosophy behind these schools would not serve in any way to the well-being of the undivided nation. The minority communities, perhaps, owing to the fear complex instituted schools competing keenly with the majority community. Ambedkar drew attention to these vicious symptoms in 'a dispassionate analysis of Hindu-Muslim relations'. He found that both communities 'obsessively considered almost every issue on how it affected them in their struggle against thc other Hindus and Muslims, he noted, make preparations with diabolical intentions against each other without abatement reminding one of a race in armaments between two hostile nations. If the Hindus have the Benares University the Muslims must have the Aligarh university. If the Hindus start the Shuddhi movement, the Muslims must launch the Tablig movement. If the Hindus start Sangathan, the Muslims must have the Tanjim" (*The Hindu*, July 9, 2002).

Set against the background of disharmony, discord and distrust, it was natural for the vulnerable minority community to be distraught as they listened to Mountbattan and the national leaders' speeches announcing partition. The news shook them out of their complacency giving them a feeling of fear and therefore "each family instinctively drew its members together, as a gesture of protection against the danger" (p. 66).

The pensive reflections of the minorities against partition find an expression in the point of view of Lala Kanshi Ram and of Arun. Their observations on the historical necessity of partition, on the idiocy and incompetence of all the national leaders, and on their failure to conceive the consequences of partition are revealing. Sometimes the arguments of Kanshi Ram and his son Arun seem to be confused, their thoughts muddled, their judgement smack of historical veracity. But then the national leaders succumbed to the same human frailties, and even more, as they were desperately struggling to find some way out. The Britishers also wanted to discover some solution to the communal tangle though they failed miserably to come to grips with it.

However, Kanshi Ram was very suspicious of the moves and motives of the British. He told his wife that "the British would rather divide than leave behind a united India" (p. 39). They maintained that if the Indian political leaders failed to arrive at some solution they would hand power over to any constituted 'authority or authorities' of the moment. It was the reference to the plural that disturbed him most. Kanshi Ram's fears may be likened to those of a student belonging to Muslim League during those fateful days. The student said to another villager (in the novel, *Aadha Gaon* (half a village by Rahi Masoom Raza).

"You must all be aware that at the present time, throughout the country, the Muslims are engaged in a life and death struggle for existence. We live in a country where our position is no more than equivalent to that of salt in dal. Once the protective shadow of the British is removed, the Hindus will devour us. That is the reason that Indian Muslims require a place where they will be able to live with honour."

However, Kanshi Ram could not trust them because the British, given to their litigious tendencies, they could encourage disunity at the expense of Hindus and Muslims. That they could remain was largely because they successfully played off one community against the other. He called up Gandhi's observation when the latter had visited Sialkot.

> The British had played the different religious groups against each other to their advantage. (p. 106)

In Sialkot, too, the British set the scene for division by encouraging different denominational schools established purely on religious lines. Arun suspected 'the parochial distinctions' were the offshoots of Britishers' machinations.

However, the novelist clearly shows that the situation on the eve of partition was so messy and volatile that no one should be blamed squarely. Undoubtedly the British had pursued the policy of divide and rule to prop up their rule. But after the Second World War they were ill at ease at home. They wanted to set India free and believed that "the greatest legacy that the British could leave was a united India."[6] The novelist appears to say that it was not the British but the national leaders of all hues whose bigoted views precipitated the country into a state of no return. Muhamad Ali Jinnah threw light on the internecine disputes among the parties which pushed the country to the precipice of partition. He remarked to a British official, 'In India we divide and you rule.' Davidson, a Britisher, and an intimate friend to Arun and Munir, opined that the Indian leaders threw many proposals away intended to keep India united. Moreover, they could not see the merit in Cabinet Mission proposals. Kanshi Ram also lambasted the leaders who had rejected every proposal which would make a united India possible. He made incisive criticism on Gandhi-Rajaji offer to Jinnah and on its pernicious results. The offer which accepted Pakistan in principle turned out to be detrimental for united India. Kanshi Ram reflected:

> Didn't Gandhiji and Rajaji themselves as much as offer Pakistan to Jinnah in 1944. They were the ones who put the idea in his head. Take a section in the East of India and a section in the West, they said. (p. 40)

What Kanshi Ram said is steeped in historical veracity. Rajaji was the first Congress leader to have seen the inevitability of Pakistan. In his eagerness to offer some solution to the communal question he made the Madras Legislature accept a resolution accepting Pakistan in principle. When it was submitted to the All-India Congress Committee, the members to a man were opposed to it. But Rajagopalachari did not give up his efforts. He brought Gandhi and Jinnah to the negotiating table. The talks failed but they improved Jinnah's bargaining position considerably. Kanshi Ram found fault with Gandhi who "by going to him [Jinnah] not only gave Pakistan a name, he gave Jinnah a name too" (p. 40). The author seems to believe that the Rajaji offer put Jinnah on the pedestal in the Muslim provinces.

Lala Kanshi Ram could not understand the somersault that Gandhi had taken with regard to partition. He was of the view that other leaders might evade the onus of keeping the country united, but Gandhi had a moral responsibility, an inner voice to justify his actions. Moreover, Gandhi asserted repeatedly that he would "never accept that" (p. 40). All the minorities were enraged when they had been informed about partition. Babi Amaravathi, the landlady of Kanshi Ram, was so bitter and when she came to know about the assassination of Gandhi, she was quick to add without a shadow of sympathy.

> It's good he is. He ruined us. (p. 362)

Little did the minorities know about the manner with which Mountbatten, with all his persuasive powers, had worked out the scheme of partition for them. In fact, Gandhi withdrew from the negotiations on partition for he felt "defeated and forsaken"[7] when he was told that Patel and Nehru had become votaries of partition. Kanshi Ram could not understand how Gandhi with secular credentials conducted himself in the manner when communal fascism, on his own admission, was staring in the face. All the important leaders and people began to ask for partition and this rendered Gandhi helpless. In this context, Bipin Chandra aptly said:

> It was the Hindus' and Sikhs' desire for partition that rendered him ineffective, blind and important. The Muslims already considered him their enemy. There were no forces of good which Gandhi would seize upon to build up a programme.[8]

In fact, his teachings of non-violence and religious tolerance which had long been upheld, by and large, were on the wane in the climate reeking with communalism.

Nahal is hard on Nehru whose speech on partition over radio created a flutter in the hearts of the minorities. For Kanshi Ram it seemed highly ridiculous when Nehru said, after partition, that the leaders were ready to make sacrifices. His speech was distanced from reality because he promised the minorities peace and protection. The minorities had nagging doubts about their future long before partition. After the announcement of it, their chances of survival if stayed in Pakistan were beyond hope. So Kanshi Ram reproved Nehru for making fatuous statements.

> Had he gone mad? Didn't he know his people? Didn't he know Muslims? And why the partition in the first place? What of your promises to us, you Pandit Nehru. (p. 65)

By the repeated use of the marks of interrogation, the novelist emphatically holds that Nehru failed to evaluate the predicament of the minorities in the newly formed states. He made it clear that the minorities were very reluctant to the idea of partition.

Nahal exposes the gross stupidity on the part of the national leaders who failed miserably to understand the communal dynamics. Of these leaders, Kripalani was considered 'the worst offender' because he asked the minorities to stay where they were. Kanshi Ram felt that the national leaders should have devised means of mass migration before rushing headlong to partition.

Nahal is highly critical of Jinnah's two-nation theory and seems to aver that the Muslims did not constitute a separate race. The leaguers used all their charm to dissuading the Muslims into believing that Hindus were different, an alien race. Little did they know the fact that the lower middle class Muslims belonging to Hinduism in the remote past had converted to Islam. Nahal states the case of Abdul Ghani, a hookah manufacturer, who was blind to the "historical truth that he was the product of many crosses between the low caste Hindu women and Moghul foot soldiers" (p. 51). But in the heat of his daily labour, he could not see the truth of it.

Nahal shows that the two-nation theory is wrong because it did not put an end to the problem of minorities for the sub-continent was a hopeless demographic mix of the two communities. Kanshi Ram contemplated:

> One would have to go around with tweezers through all the villages to separate the Muslims from the Hindus. (p. 96)

There was a Muslim in every corner of undivided India where there was a Hindu. If the rationale behind the creation of Pakistan is argued, there could be no place for minorities anywhere. Having been driven out of Pakistan, Kanshi Ram thought that his position was positively different in the free India because he belonged to the majority community. But, to his dismay, he found that he belonged to a new minority of refugees. The cup of their misery was full when Arun, all agog, was rushing home thinking that some riot would break out in the city, New Delhi. "If not the Muslims, the Punjabi refugees might be attacked" (p. 365). In fact, Pakistan created new minorities and it presumably aggravated the condition of minorities by making it a permanent feature in the politics of the subcontinent.

After partition everyone began to view others in terms of religion. The tenor of Arun and Nur's love, for instance, underwent sea-change as both of them were suddenly conscious of their being a Hindu and a Muslim. Arun who had long been resolved to switch over to Islam all of a sudden became impatient and irrational. When Nur asked him whether he would become a Muslim for her sake, Arun curtly retorted in a vein of sarcasm:

> Why should I become a Muslim? Why shouldn't you? That is, if you love me. Why shouldn't you become a Hindu? (p. 111)

In fact, in the sickening climate of communal bitterness and hatred even 'the pure and profound Arun-Nur love-relationship ceases to be a private, personal affair, and in spite of them it comes to acquire communal or political overtones."[9] Symbolically the parting of the lovers coincides with the partition of the nation.

The holocaust that followed partition was "unforeseen in magnitude, unreasoned in savagery and unordered in pattern."[10] As Kanshi Ram was grieved by the sad turn of events taking place in Sialkot he was informed that his daughter and son-in-law were killed in a train tragedy. Chaman Nahal's sister was done away with the same brutality. He writes: "My sister had been assassinated near Wazirabad—another psychological reason for us to get away from the neighbourhood as quickly as possible" (*Across Border*). He felt insecure, forlorn and unprotected. His wife, Probharani was certain that Sialkot was no city for the Hindus. Even Kanshi Ram, who was very fond of Sialkot and was ready to forgo his religion for the privilege of allowing him to stay in the city, saw how defenseless he himself was, with all his friends in the Muslim community and with the police. He insisted that they should leave for India at the earliest possible occasion. They enlisted their names in a convoy which had a strength of over twenty thousand people.

The immediate impact of partition was on the silent minority who were uprooted from home and field and driven by sheer fear of death to seek safety across a line they had neither drawn nor desired. Partition uprooted the minorities of Sialkot from their homes and hearths and left them utterly helpless as the Muslims were hell-bent on causing as much trouble as they could. However, the convoy was slowly winding its way towards the Indian border. They continued the journey with blistered foot as the Muslim marauders mauled the convoy of refugees across the newly formed state. Theirs was a trek with each mile menaced with exhaustion, starvation, cholera and other physical infirmities. In fact, they passed through 'a living inferno' littered with dismembered human limbs, corpses, skeletons and discarded clothes. By the time they rode out of the storm they were only a demoralised mass of humanity. As a refugee of partition, Chaman Nahal underwent the whole agony. He reflected:

> I was born in Sialkot and after 1947 we were driven away to India. I can understand the suffering and loneliness that such an exile imposes on the persons involved in a class by itself."[11]

The survival of the refugees was under constant threat and there was often no defence against the Muslims for the police were hand in glove with the miscreants.

Chaman Nahal maintains remarkable aesthetic distance in the presentation of points of view which are plausibly poised. His narration of the gruesome horrors of partition in which the Muslims and the Hindus were victimised was also free from bias. Though he is a Hindu and was a victim of partition, it does not warp his sensibility and he blames all the warring communities. He shows violence came to a crescendo in Sialkot only with the trickle of the Muslim refugees pouring in the city with their tell-tales of suffering and woe. It is obvious that they had been attacked and were driven out of their homes by their counterparts, the Hindus and the Sikhs in the eastern part of Punjab. Like the Muslims in Pakistan, the Hindus and the Sikhs, too, wallowed in arson, murder, rape and others. On his way to Delhi, Kanshi Ram saw a train with hundreds of slaughtered Muslims. Bands of suspicious people belonging to Hindu and Sikh communities appeared at the wayside stations waiting to pounce upon the Muslim refugees. At Amritsar, the members of Kanshi Ram's family came across a procession of Muslim women paraded nakedly through the bazaar. It may be likened to the naked procession of Hindu women at Narrowal in Pakistan. Nahal describes all the excruciating details with compelling vividness with remarkable disinterestedness. As a refugee of partition, Chaman Nahal has given away to despair and grief. He had a close call while fleeing from Pakistan to India: "These was incessant rain all the way and we were obliged to spend the night in a barn en route, only a few miles away from Pakistan. Throughout the night we heard beating of drums and other sounds coming from that direction. Residents in the area had been attacked and butchered, the hostile mobs from over there could as well do the same to us" (*Across Borders*).

On watching the terror let loose by the Hindus and the Sikhs, Kanshi Ram, who had long been nourishing hatred against the Muslims, felt qualms of conscience. He "ceased to hate" (p. 338) Muslims because Hindus were equally guilty. O.P. Mathur says:

> Lala Kanshi Ram thus takes a stance which clearly demonstrates his freedom from commitment to anything except love, compassion and tolerance which alone makes political freedom more meaningful.[12]

Now he wanted to lead a life free from malice and rancour. Hatred drags down the soul and defiles it. To attain purity of soul, he has to avoid hatred at all costs. In a way he loves the sinner and seeks to draw him from his sin and to himself.

Chaman Nahal discloses the miserable state of the new minority-refugees who could not justify their presence anywhere. Kanshi Ram hoped that the refugees would be given red-carpet treatment. He was on of the horns of the dilemma when the local people at Delhi resented the presence of the refugees. But Kanshi Ram did not give in. He made all desperate efforts to find some refugee flat. To his dismay, the Area Custodian of Evacuee Property demanded bribe, the amount which was beyond his means. It was as if he had, awakened from a bad dream to worse reality. He felt utterly defeated and exposed. Chaman Nahal shares his bitter memories in his article entitled Across Borders brought out in *The Hindustan Times*, May 11, 1997. His memories are more poignant and touching than those of his fictional creations. He reminisces:

> "There are two ogres one has always to face before stepping into the paradisal unknown; the immigration officer and the custom officer. Never have I seen suspicion lurking so forcefully in anyone other than these menaces. For them, every person is a dodger and a criminal and they give you a mean eye before you have placed your documents in front of them...I have just returned home having been bruised and humiliated in many such encounters with them yet again."

Towards the close of the aftermath, Arun found his father, Kanshi Ram, weeping. "Never before his life had he felt so exposed, so naked, so defenceless" (p. 350). The jolt he received in India was so intense, its repercussions were so deep that he stopped wearing a turban, a symbol of dignity. It is just the kind of experience that partition might be expected to create.

> A turban was a sign of respect of dignity. He had no dignity left. (p. 366)

Kanshi Ram's feelings may be equated with Saadat Hasan Manto who authored Siyah Hashyre, an objective portrayal of the partition holocaust. Manto went to Pakistan in January 1948. He was sad at leaving a city where he had spent many working days of his life. 'Bombay,' he wrote, 'had asked me no questions It had taken me to its generous bosom, me, a man rejected by his family, a gypsy, by temperament... After leaving Bombay, I was sad. My friends of whom I was proud were in Bombay. It was there that I married. My first child was born in that city...In Bombay I earned from a few hundred to several thousand rupees and spent them all. I was in love with Bombay. I still am (Mishirul Hasan's *India Partitioned* p. 29).

The story on the other side of the border to which Kanshi Ram joyously turned, was the same. Initially the local inhabitants of Pakistan were most kindly disposed towards the new arrivals from India, calling them Muhajir (literally meaning migrant) after the refugees who had accompanied the prophet Muhammad to Medina. However, once the fear of Hindu domination was gone, internal rivalries and tensions emerged between the incoming refugees and the local residents.

'The psychological impact' of partition on the lives of the refugees had far-reaching results. The immediate result of their (Kanshi Ram and others) coming over to Delhi was the loss of personality and of identity. He found himself before a long tunnel where he could not see the other end. To top it all, Lala Kanshi Ram and the members of his family found themselves completely at a loss of contact and of communication with each other. They could not share their feelings, nor put their thoughts into words which were too meagre to convey their anguish.

> The three of them lay fully awake. Not being able to fathom their minds and feeling restless about it. Not being able to talk to each other and feeling guilty about it. (p. 370)

The loss of communication throws them into a vortex of complete isolation and alienation, and making each a prisoner of his own single self. Mir Taqi Mir, a great Urdu poet, who could not bear to be away from Delhi even for a short while, was compelled to leave it. He strikes a melancholy note when he says:

> What matters it, o breeze
>
> If now has come the spring
>
> When I have lost them both
>
> The garden and my nest.

This process of isolation, whether expansive or narrow, is productive of confusion, conflict and sorrow unleashed by partition tragedy.

In the end of the novel, the evil, the futility and the stupidity of hatred have been shown by the whirring of Sunanda's machine, a symbol of creative action and unfailing hope. She suffered a lot. She was brutally raped and lost her husband in the riots in Pakistan; she was made poor. Despite all these pains, it is she who makes a final gesture of endurance in the novel.

> The machine went whirring on, its wheel turning fast and its needle moving up and down murmuring and sewing through the cloth. (p. 371)

The initiative now passes into the hands of the individual. She is no longer a passive victim but can stitch out her own destiny. Love and creative action as evidenced in the lives of Kanshi Ram and Sunanda respectively are all the supreme values which form the moving drama of violence and malevolence. Without love collective action is merely compulsion, breeding antagonism and fear, from which arise private and social conflicts. Through self knowledge alone is there freedom from bondage, and this freedom is devoid of all beliefs, all ideologies.

Since Nahal's concerns are not only the socio-economic and humanistic implications of partition, but also the deep psychic disturbances and emotional transformations, the usual narrative methods would not have suited his purpose. He has, therefore, employed what may be called multiple or shifting points of view. It is Kanshi Ram and Arun's points of view which form the major part of the novel. The mixing up of points of view of the protagonist, Kanshi Ram and that of Arun in the main seems not to destroy the unity of impression. When political exigencies take control of events characters tend to become inferior to the works of art. However, Nahal harnesses the point of view to characters so as to amplify the personality of the characters. It may be said that Nahal employs this technique which helps him overcome a limited vision.

Nahal's *Azadi* seems to be different from all the other partition novels in that it makes an effort to encompass all the evils that partition has brought forth. It does not terminate with the minorities fleeing to India. Perhaps the novelist seeks to continue the plot in India in order to catch the ominous effects of the aftermath on the lives of a few individuals in particular. The novel seems to be very significant because here Nahal's vision is very expansive which enables his protagonist to cease hating his counterparts in Pakistan. Indeed, in its probe into historical complexities, in its capturing the delicate feelings of the minority of refugees, and in its attempt to grasp their trauma, *Azadi* proves to be a classic. As "the comprehensive fictional accounts of the partition holocaust"[13] and as "a novel of epical dimensions"[14] the novel appears to be unrivalled.

REFERENCES

1. R.K. Dhawan: *Three Contemporary Novelists* (New Delhi: Classical Publishing Company, 1985), p. 73.
2. Bipin Chandra: *Communalism in Modern India* (New Delhi: Vikas Publishing Pvt. Ltd., 1987) p. 154.
3. Chaman Nahal: *Azadi* (New Delhi: Orient Paperbacks, 1975), p. 1. Further references to this text in this chapter will be cited parenthetically by page number.
4. Mishirul Hasan: *Nationalism and Communal Politics in India* (New Delhi: Manohar Publications, 1994), p. 78.
5. Bipin Chandra: *Communalism in Modern India*, p. 198.
6. Peter Heehs: *India's Freedom Struggle* (Delhi: Oxford University Press, 1988), p. 155.
7. Tara Chand: *History of Freedom Movement in India* (New Delhi: Ministry of Information and Broadcasting Publication Division, 1977), p. 518.
8. Bipin Chandra: *India's Struggle for Freedom* (Delhi: Penguin, 1987), p. 318.
9. R.K. Dhawan: *Three Contemporary Novelists*, p. 72.

10. Larry Collins and Dominique Lapierre *Freedom at Midnight* (New Delhi: Vikas Publishing House Pvt. Ltd., 1975), p. 284.
11. R.K. Dhawan: *Three Contemporary Novelists*, p. 96.
12. Madhusudan Prasad (Ed.): *Indian-English Novelists: Chaman Nahal* by O.P. Mathur (New Delhi: Sterling Publishers Pvt. Ltd., 1982), p. 89.
13. M.K. Naik: *A History of Indian-English Literature* (New Delhi: Sahitya Academy, 1982), p. 331.
14. Madhusudan Prasad (Ed.): *Indian-English Novelists: Chaman Nahal* by O.P. Mathur, p. 89.

Tamas

Tamas was written by Bhisham Sahni in Hindi and was translated into English by Jai Rajan after a lapse of nearly three decades. Though it was a translated work, the ethos and the distinctive quality of the original are carried into the English version. Its author, Bhisham Sahni, was born in 1915 into a devout Arya Samajist family in Rawalpindi (now in Pakistan). Having completed schooling there, he went to Government College, Lahore, from where he took Master's degree in English Literature. He returned to Rawalpindi to join his father's import business but, finding the job too taxing, decided to teach at a local college. At the same time he also became involved in the activities of the Indian National Congress. After partition in 1947, Sahni's family opted to settle in India and he took the last train to India. He settled down in Delhi where he is teaching at a Delhi University college. In 1957 he moved to Moscow to work as a translator and returned to India in 1963 to resume teaching.

Sahni first collection of short stories, *Bhagya Rekha* (Line of Fate) won him name and fame. He edited a literary journal, *Naya Kahaniyam* for some time. So far he has published five novels, eight collection of short stories, three plays and a biography. Many of his books have been translated into various languages. His novel, *Tamas,* was based on his personal experiences as a young man when he himself had to work as a relief officer after partition. The tragedy of the people had moved him greatly and made him realise the harsh realities of life.

Thus while supporting a progressive and scientific approach to social phenomena, he has developed a deep faith in humanism. There is an integration of both a traditional and non-traditional world-view to be found in his work. His intellectual orientation as can be seen from the novel was largely refined by Marxism, Gandhian philosophy and the positive side of existentialism.

Tamas, as an anatomy of partition, depicts how communal violence was generated by fundamentalists in the three communities and how innocent persons were duped into serving the ulterior purposes of the communalists, who infused tension and hatred for their own ends at the cost of intercommunal harmony. As the title *Tamas* suggests, it is an attempt to depict and condemn the ignorance and darkness involved in communal violence on the eve of the partition of India. A good number of episodes, dealing with communal mayhem during the pre-partition days, are interspersed in the novel to show how communal madness stalked the northern parts of the sub-continent. The first episode of the novel is the killing of a pig which sparked off riots when it was thrown on the steps of a mosque at the instance of a Muslim Leaguer, Murad Ali. The other episodes, silhouetted against this backdrop, are intended to show how the tentacles of communalism spread to the rural areas. The novelist makes it clear that it was the onus of the three communities—Hindus, Muslims and Sikhs—who had unabashedly perpetrated arson, rape, murder, conversions in the name of religion. The novelist seems to interpret the evil designs of the British and of the communal groups mainly through Richard, an I.C.S.

The conversation between Richard and his wife Liza introduces the theme of partition. Their conversation proves the fact that the policy of divide and rule wrought havoc by making the people alienated and grew suspicious of one another and became suddenly blind as communal passions took hold of them. The British were mainly accountable for the growth of communalism because though they knew well that "the Indians are an irascible lot and highly volatile...ready to shed blood in the name of religion...,[1] they played the part of a spectator wantonly watching the warring communities.

Richard, the highest official of the district, became "the mouth-piece of British imperialism when he took upon himself the task of putting into practice the policies and imperialist designs of the British ruling class" (p. 40). With an intention to save the empire at any cost they began to play off one community against the other. Obviously, no one can say that there was not an inherent tendency towards the division in India and with the prospect of the approach of political power, this was likely to grow. It was possible to tone down this tendency; it was also possible to accentuate it. The government adopted the latter policy and encouraged every fissiparous tendency in the country to safeguard the empire and themselves. This is clear when Richard said to his wife:

> When the people fight among, themselves the ruler is safe. (p. 45).

The conversation between Liza and Richard reveals that the British rulers did play an important role in the promotion, spread, growth and ultimate success of communalism. Their role became crucial precisely because they held the state power which was a crucial determinant. They could prevent Indians from fighting in the name of religion. This was clearly told with great candour by Bakshiji when he curtly said to Richard, "Everything is under you, Saheb. If only you have a mind to...". But Richard was quick to add in high-handed manner that the problem should be brought before Pandit Nehru or Baldev Singh. The fact is that he was totally reluctant to keep the city under control because, as he explained to Liza, if they joined hands and fought against them, the Britishers and the empire would be at great peril.

It should be remembered in this context that "the communal division was not the only constituent of the policy of divide and rule just as divide and rule was the only weapon in the armoury of colonialism for its preservation and continuance."[2] Every effort was made to set as many groups and interests against one another to find and widen as many social gaps as possible; and different permutations and combinations were tried at different times to split up the Indian people and prevent their emerging unity. Sahni shows this when Richard said that Indians "came from the same stock." (p. 53) He did know that Indians knew nothing about it. He did not want to make Indians know these facts because "the rulers don't look for similarities among the ruled. They are only interested in finding out what can keep them apart" (p. 42). As can be seen from the novel that divide and rule was, for the British, a many-splendoured policy. Sahni shows how the element of communalism had been exploited by the British for they knew that communal division could survive to the end and was the most serviceable.

Tamas ruthlessly shows that "if people who do not know history are perhaps condemned—as Santayana puts it—they are certainly prone to repeat it."[3] This becomes clear in the conversation between Richard and Liza. Basically, the Indians, whether Muslims or Indians, are one nation—their roots were the same. Richard emphatically said:

> The first lot came from central Asia...And those that followed after a lapse of many centuries were also from the same stock. Their origin, so to speak, was the same. The first bunch were known as the Aryans. They came into this country thousands of years ago. The others who were known as Mussalmans made inroads into this country thousand years ago. But their roots were the same. (pp. 36-37)

The Indians in whose memories history and myth were so often blurred had only observed the difference. The ethos of a race or a nation is a continuum, it is rooted in the past, it shapes the present, and is an inspiration for the future. But the people were ignorant of these facts because "they don't know their history. They only live it" (p. 37). Their gross ignorance about the present was even more gaping than their blindness to history. This is brought out clearly when Richard explained to his wife about the fundamental oneness of the Indians.

> Have you ever taken a good look at these people? They belong to the same stock, the same features, same noses, mouths, broad foreheads, brown eyes. (p. 36)

They took after one another so much that Liza could not distinguish between a Hindu and a Muslim. Though Richard expatiated on the subject it did not dawn upon her. In the same way Roshanlal found it very difficult to throw light on the subject. There were some outward differences among the 'people of the same stock' belonging to different religions, but these paled into insignificance when, for instance, Iqbal Singh who was converted to Sheikh Iqbal Ahmed before nobody could find the difference because the fanatics obliterated the signs of Iqbal Singh's Sikhism; "in their place were all external Muslim signs" (p. 152).

Malcolm Darling in his inspection report 1945 during his tour of the Punjab made keen observation on the changing pattern of relationships particularly in villages. "If only propaganda had not poisoned the air with hatred and distrust, Hindu, Muslim and Sikh could have continued to live happily together in the village, as they had done for over a hundred years...we met Muslims who for generations had their genealogies kept and horoscopes cast by Brahmins, and passed villages owned by Muslim and Sikh, or by Hindu and Muslim, sprung from a common ancestor and we even came across one village where Hindu, Muslim and Sikh were of the same tribe. Without good-neighbourliness there can be no comfort in village life, but alas, propaganda with its ghastly brood—mutilation, massacre and rape—has turned Jinnah's two-nation creed in the village from a theory into a bloody fact."

Sahni throws into bold relief that people hailing from the same community were different. It is ironical to note that Murad Ali, who was a notorious communist and the one behind the spate of communal violence, was dark, thick-set, short-statured...small penetrating eyes in stark contrast to Shahnawaz, who was the voice of sanity helping his Hindu brethren during riots, was 'a portly man, broad chested' and handsome. Milkhi, a Brahmin, was a 'dirty, slimy lizard'. 'Nobody knew his origins.' What Mushirul Hasan has said is worth mentioning:

> The obvious fact that the Indian Muslims do not constitute a single, homogeneous and monolithic entity and the differentiating features that characterise Indian society are also to be found within the Muslim community.[4]

Thus Sahni debunks the falsity of Jinnah's two-nation theory insinuating that people belonging to the self-same religion had diverse racial origins. Despite their conversion to Islam Muslims refer to themselves as Jats, Gujjars, Rajputs, etc. This is specially so during match-making in an arranged *nikah* (marriage). One instance of the visibility of casteist feelings among Pakistanis is the reference Benazir Bhutto makes in her book *Daughter of the East*, when she says, 'In my veins runs the blood of a Wadhera.' Wadheras are a Rajput clan from Punjab and Sindh. The Sikhs too refer to themselves as Jat Sikhs, Majabhi Sikhs, etc., Raj Sikhs profess surnames like Chauhan (Jagjit Singh Chauhan), (Ganga Singh Dhillon), Arora, Oberoi, Sainai, etc., that display caste backgrounds. Caste wheedles its way into most religions in India. However, the social inequalities in other religions are not so stark as in Hinduism.

Co-existence and interdependence are the marked features of the town. 'There was hardly any wedding in the city which Khudha Baksh had not stitch the bridal cloths.'(sic). The intimacy between the close friends, Raghunadh and Shahnawaz, was very warming and touching to observe during the riot. Raghunadh's wife did not veil herself before Shahnawaz. She did not observe *purdah* and she affectionately called him 'Khanji.' Even Congress and Muslim League leaders were prone to exchange pleasantries with great warmth of feeling when they were together. Thus "the multifarious activities of the people, like the measured tones of a symphony, were attuned to the heart-beat of the city" (p. 88). In general, integrative and syncretic forces were at work both at the popular and the elite level, though their progress was impeded by stray localized and sporadic incidence of conflict over religious symbols.

When the Congress movement was started, it 'created ripples disturbing the even tenor of the city.' In the same way, the procession taken out by Sikhs on the birthday of Guru Nanak gave anxious moments to the people. They watched with bated breath to see whether the procession would abstain from playing music as it passed along the Jama Masjid, or whether stones would be hurled at the procession out of wanton provocation. Similarly people were on tenterhooks when the Muslims took out processions and went through the bazaars. On such occasions the fear of communal violence might come true. Thus "people's mutual relationships and those of the various communities, constituting the totality of humanity, were precariously poised" (p. 89).

The main thrust in *Tamas* is the grim consequences of communal politics leading to partition. Glorifying the past leaders on communal lines, and associating religious symbols with party politics caused a ripple effect eating into the very structure of society. Though often adopting diametrically opposite and hostile positions, the communal interpretation of history adopted basically the same historiographic framework, premises and assumptions. Often, the only difference was that the other community was the culprit. Quite often, in the hands of the communalist, the entire treatment of the past was allegorical. In the novel, Vanprasthiji, a Hindu priest, chanted the couplet.

> Horrible have been the sins of the Muslims in the land
>
> Even the sky has refused us its favour and the earth its bountry. (p. 57)

The crisis was being used to serve divergent political objectives. The priest-craft sought to use it to appropriate it for a harmful cause.

Similarly, "the Sikhs believed that they were settling scores with their traditional enemies, the same Turks" (p. 193). It became most virulent with Muslims. "It's the age-old enmity between the Hindu and the Muslim. A kafir is a kafir. As long as he does not profess the right religion, he will remain our enemy. To kill a kafir brings merit" (p. 168). Their minds had been conditioned by the propaganda. It is highly difficult for them to rid themselves of it because as J. Krishna Murthy says, "one has to be sufficiently attentive to see the whole significance of this conditioning, how it divides people, nationally, religiously, socially, linguistically. These divisions are a tremendous barrier; they breed conflict and violence."

Thus it was assumed or implied that whatever had happened then was bound to happen now and, therefore, contemporary politics were projected into the past and the happenings of the past were so described as to serve the communal politics. The three communities adopted an interpretation of the past, through which feelings of fear, insecurity and isolation could be aroused among the people of the present. In the sense, while communal history produced and propagated communalism, in the turn communal politics gave a fillip to alienation.

The communalist primarily saw medieval Indian history as one long story of Hindu-Muslim conflict. Hindus and Muslims were permanently divided into separate camps whose mutual relations were bitter, distrustful and hostile. This indoctrination seeped in the minds of the teenagers during their impressionable age. Master Devbrat trained up Ranvir, a Brahmin, to kill a hen thereby enabling him to possess a stout heart. He was waiting for the enemy and was ready to bid his followers to pounce upon the enemy. He "imagined Shjivaji would have paced outside his tent before throwing the gallant soldiers into battle against Aurangzeb" (p. 137). Similarly when the Muslim rioters were about to attack Gurudwara, the Sikhs, having amassed arsenals overnight singing in unison, thought:

> Three hundred years ago, they had sung they same song before going to meet the enemy. (p. 161)

This struggle or hostility between the Hindus, Sikhs on one side and the Muslims on the other was then, according to the communal view, naturally carried over to the twentieth century and served as the basis or the cause as well as justification for the current communal antagonism. The remedies to the communal problem put forth by them were very similar. While the Muslim communalists raised the demand for the separation of Muslims from Hindus through the creation of Pakistan, the Hindu communalists demanded the expulsion or the subordination of Muslims who had refused to be absorbed and had therefore remained foreigners.

Religion was brought in actively during the mass, fascist phase of communalism when it was used to mobilize the common people. People came to the revered Vanprasthiji not for religious reasons. After the service was over, the members of the congregation continued to sit to listen to the communal speeches by religious leaders. 'They had a readymade topic. The highly charged communal tensions in the city.' In his 'sermon' Vanprasthiji referred to the sins of the Muslims in the land in a couplet. He asked the Hindus 'to have a canister of mustard oil and a sack of charcoal ready at hand' to pour over the enemies, because the Muslims 'had been collecting lathis, spears and such other lethal weapons in the Jama Masjid.' Temple bell was repaired at once to alarm the people in case of trouble. The same was the case with Sikhs who were very aggressive and petulant. Partition was bound to give a deadly blow particularly when it comes to Sikhs. The Punjab was multilated into two parts. The birth of the two provinces was just like 'sundering apart of a complex living organism into two' which were destined to lead a precarious dead-alive existence for a long time to come. On June 14, 1947 Lord Mountbatten's press attache wrote: "We are in the heart of Sikh country here and the prevailing atmosphere is one of tension and forbidding. They (the Sikhs) see that the partition of India means substantially and irrevocably the partition of the Sikhs." (*Indian Punjab* by Dr. B.S. Nijjar). Sardar Teja Singh and others gathered people together at Gurudwara to announce in prayer.

> The Khalsa, the pure heart will dominate the world. The enemy will be annihilated. (p. 165)

Like the Sikhs, the Muslim inhabitants of the village "had overnight turned into crusaders and were preparing to earn merit by killing infidels" (p. 163).

Religiosity is a major contributory factor, as seen from the above, and, at the popular plane, imparted communalism the passion and intensity which made it politically effective. Religiosity may be defined as "deep and intense emotional commitment to matters of religion and religious emotions intrude into non-religious or non-spiritual areas of life."[5] As Nehru pointed out, there was 'too much religiosity in India.'

That religion played, in communalism, an entirely extraneous or vicarious role—the role of mask—is clearly brought out if one takes a look at the religious side of the communal leaders in the novel. Ramjan and Murad Ali, for example, are not orthodox or even practising Muslims. To them the Islamic appeal is simply an instrument of rabble rousing. So is the case with Ranvir and Teja Singh. In fact Nathu who, in his innocence, slew the pig at the behest of Murad Ali and became, though indirectly, the cause of rioting in the city, is more religious for he took it to heart when he came to know how he had been used as a decoy.

In the long and impressive history of India's nationalist movement there was a deep ideological schism between ardent communal nationalist and committed champions of a secular and composite Indian state. The same pattern can be seen in the city which was but a microcosm of the national arena of Indian politics where the battlelines were clearly demarcated and the Leaguers in particular were not in a mood to relent. As a secular party it was the onus of the Congress party to dispel fears in the Muslims. Time and again the leaders of Muslim League emphasised that Congress belonged to the Hindus and 'Muslims have nothing to do with it' and as such it could not look after the interests of the Muslims. The allegation was not far from truth. Most of the Congress leaders were the members of the Hindu Mahasabha too. Bakshiji, a true Gandhiite, warned Mahatmaji.

> It doesn't behove a man to put his legs in two boats. But you have been doing just that all your life. One leg in the Congress and the other in the Hindu Mahasabha boat. (p. 79)

This political opportunism tended to orientate Muslims towards a communal outlook with the feeling that the success of such a national movement led by Congress would mean a Hindu supremacy in Indian politics. There were 'only a handful of Muslims' with Congress. Of these, 'except for Muzaffar, no Muslim wears a Gandhi cap.' To make matters worse, some Congress leaders were so suspicious of Congress Muslims that they would like to maintain 'some distance.' Sardar Bishan Singh 'had no compunction in working' with Hakimji, a Congress Muslim. During the riot some Congress Muslims left the Congress saying that Hindus were behind the throwing the pig on the steps of the mosque. The bickerings in the party on every issue taken, without any ideological basis, are indicative of loss of Gandhian values. The novel, indeed, is a successful exposition of the failure of Gandhian ideals. This is clearly evidenced in the speech between Bakshiji and Mahatmaji. When Bakshiji demonstrated with him to keep away from the Hindu Mahasabha, Mehataji was quick to retort.

> If trouble breaks out, will you come to my rescue?...If trouble comes will...Bapuji come to my help? (p. 79)

However, Bakshiji and the General stood their ground and did not forsake Gandhian ideals. In troubled times their integrity had been tested and they did not succumb under pressure. Though Bakshiji was called a 'Hindu dog,' he remained calm. The General was struck to death when he harangued on the importance of living in amity during riots. They offered supreme sacrifice in the face of overwhelming odds.

Sahni demonstrates that the historical incident became a pretext for the evil in human minds to manifest itself. Soon after the killing of the pig thrown on the steps of the mosque, a Muslim was after a cow inclined to kill it. On watching the events Bakshiji remarked, "Soon vultures and kites will fly over the city." The prophecy came true and soon the city was on flames. "The flames licked upward like the red fangs of a mighty snake gradually spreading" (p. 110). Inder who was in his tender age killed a perfume seller on Ranvir's instructions. Harman Singh's shop was looted and set ablaze. His daughter, along with the other Sikh women, jumped into the well as the marauders began to siege the Gurudwara. His son, Iqbal Singh, was circumcised and was converted to Islam. Many poor people cutting across religious lines were ruthlessly butchered. Rioting, arson, murder and forced conversions went on unabated for a few days. When riots came to a grinding halt, two refugee camps were set up to take care of the uprooted people of the twenty villages in the area. These were the horrors let loose during the pre-partition days, which would find a more vigorous, dehumanized expression during the times of partition.

'The Hindu-Muslim riots in the Punjab were,' remarks Prem Raman Uprety, 'people's riots, that is to say, the participants were common men walking in the streets of towns and villages or taking part in religious processions, who for a day or two or even a week would shed the role of law-abiding citizens and assume the part of looters and plunderers.' They were responding to a whole range of grievances, both economic and political, but the immediate cause is always religious. It was thus the religious fanaticism that provided a perennial source of energy that ignited the Hindu-Muslim antagonism. In a way, the communal politics were a clear manifestation of distrust and tension among the Indian leaders that was being openly expressed by the masses in a more open and physical fashion.

Bhisham Sahni's faith in Marxism and his scientific approach to social phenomena are clearly brought out. The novelist's tone is one of humanism and it is reflected in Rajo and Shahnawaz, the voices of sanity in the novel. "His impressions of the Marxist class character of society are also depicted in the novel."[6] In the riots, the poor suffered a lot because 'one always attacks a weakling.' Two college peons were engrossed discussing the offshoots of the riots. One of them observed:

> Only foolish people like us suffer in these riots. The rich and those coming from good families don't fight...Just watch them. How friendly they are with one another. (p. 231)

What Bapsi Sidhwa says on the polluted arena of politics is also worthwhile. She says, "as a Parsee, I can see things objectively. I see all the common people suffering while the politicians on either side have fun" (writer-in-Residence). It has been said that before the Second World War, the Hindus, the Muslims and the Sikhs lived, for the most part, amicably, as neighbours in rural Punjab. With the morbid propaganda which accompanied the elections of 1945-46 communal politics burst into the village setting Muslims against non-Muslims and giving both a new and exciting word—freedom.

Sahni puts the communist party on the pedestal for, it seems, he has a soft corner for it as can be seen in the elevation of character of Devdutt who tried his best to prevent the rioting and indeed has not in any way 'relaxed his efforts while riots were on.' He tried all along to get the Congress and the Muslim League to come together and devise some means of maintaining the peace at the risk of his life. When all the members were wrangling over the composition of the Peace Committee, he said:

> We must wage a war against the communal elements. It is not necessary to represent each community on the committee. The point is that the Peace Committee should take care of every interest...(p. 233)

However, it has been argued that in the struggle for freedom Marxists in India did not have a lion's share. It was alleged that the Communist Party of India, taking the cue from Russia during the Second World War and later, failed to play its destined role properly. Balbir K. Puni, in his article, 'Results from the Lab' remarks: 'Is it not ironical that the secular cabal now led by the Marxists, who in the 1930s and 40s had supplied the intellectual arguments that Jinnah needed for the creation of Pakistan and which left the sub-continent soaked in blood (*Outlook,* December 30, 2002).

Sahni has a great regard for Gandhian philosophy evidenced in the elevation of characters, the General and Bakshiji. The General took it upon himself to put a stop to the rioting and was struck to death in the process. He was a semi-illiterate, slightly eccentric but he knew what to do if somebody attacked him to give in the spirit of Gandhism. He was a symbol of Gandhi's creed of non-violence.

Sahni's vision does not augur well for humanity in the conclusion he gives to the novel. The instigator of communal violence, Murad Ali, was posing as a lover of peace. Yet Sahni too in the final analysis shows the futility and meaninglessness of hatred and malevolence. The message is loud and clear directed against the sickness of communalism which marked on the eve of the vivisection of the sub-continent.

Sahni's creativity is characterised by deep reflection upon the complexities and nuances of reality. In order to catch the very rhythm of human tragedy of great dimensions, Sahni makes use of episodic narrative which helps the author to draw a number of concentric circles of experiences and build their cumulative effect. But the episodes and the points of view in this episodic novel remain broadly similar. This denudes the novel of a possible multiple perspective on the situation. Another limitation is that the novelist leaves the threads of narrative on occasions. One does not know what happens in the incompatible relationship between Richard and Liza or in the forced conversion of Iqbal Singh into Iqbal Ahmad. Moreover, Sahni's interpretation of events following the division of the country leans more on religious grounds than on historical complexities. This deprives *Tamas* a tangled poignancy and richness. However, the perspective he offers—unbiased, objective—seems to be commendable. Govind Nihalani aptly says:

> As a novel *Tamas* is episodic in structure, which, from the point of view of literary craftsmanship may not exactly be considered flawless. Yet, as a piece of literature it reveals the vision of one detached yet passionate, quietly reflective yet emotionally intense.[7]

This is the novel which shows the dynamics of communal politics deeply entrenched at urban level insidiously worming its way into rural areas. However, its political mechanism is not independent in nature but an inalienable part and a microcosm of sectarian politics at the national level. The communal groups, which were blind to 'the same roots,' could only work and act at the behest of their communal leaders. The novel is significant because here Sahni successfully reveals how the communal leaders, in the guise of religion, pressed religious symbols into service and made battles over them. Nothing could resolve the communal tangle nor could anything restore sanity in the minds of the people as 'tamasa,' the darkness of intolerance and of communal frenzy hovers over them. The veil of darkness would not lift in the days to come during the fateful days of independence. There is indeed little hope that the baptism of freedom would be without any murky blots.

REFERENCES

1. Sahni Bisham: *Tamas* (New Delhi: Penguin Books, 1987), p. 42. Further references to this text in this chapter will be cited parenthetically by page number.
2. Bipin Chandra: *Communalism in Modern India* (New Delhi: Vikas Publishing Pvt. Ltd., 1987), p. 174.
3. Sudha Sundaram: "Partition in Historical Fiction," *The Literary Criterion*, Vol. 28, 1993, p. 78.
4. Mushirul Hasan: "In Search of Integration and Identity," *Economic and Political Weekly*, Vol. 23.
5. Bipin Chandra: *Communalism in Modern India*, p. 174.
6. Sulochana Rangeya Raghava: *Sociology of Indian Literature* (Jaipur: Rawat Publications, 1987), p. 25.
7. Sahni Bhisham: Introduction: *Tamas* by Govinda Nihalani, p. 5.

Ice-Candy Man (Cracking India)

Bapsi Sidhwa, novelist of great renown, was born in Karachi and brought up in Lahore. An active socialist among Asian women, she represented Pakistan at the Asian Women's Congress held in 1975. She has brought out three other novels, *The Crow Eaters, The Pakistani Bride* and *The American Brat*. She divides her time between the United States where she teaches and Pakistan.

Sidhwa's third novel offers a fascinating account of the violent racial-religious clashes. Initially, the novel took the name *Ice-Candy Man*. However, publishers feared that an American audience might mistake the unfamiliar name for a drug pusher. So, the title was altered to *Cracking India*. In fact the *Ice-Candy Man* is a Muslim street vendor drawn like many other men by the magnetic beauty of Ayah, Lenny's nanny (Godmother) etc. Lenny, an observant narrator, sees through the transition of the Ice-Candy Man through the roles of ice-cream vendor, bird-seller, cosmic connector to Allah via telephone, pimp. The last role shows the devious methods which some, particularly politicians, will resort to in order to survive. However, the novelist has changed the title to meaningfully suggest the vivisection of the country.

The novelist delicately threads the story of the precocious girl with the din of violence ready to crash around her world as the partition moves from political planning into reality. Like the novelist, she is stricken with polio. Many an occasion, her understanding of the cataclysm is limited by her tender age. She ponders pensively whether the earth will bleed when the adults 'crack' India. The historical scene of the partition is integrated well into the novel through Lenny's young eyes, though Sidhwa is criticised for making the character too intelligent for her age. In fact, it is through Lenny's memories that the novel gains depth and resonance.

The novel recaptures the ominous reverberations of the traumatic experience of partition after forty years. She presents a brilliant close-up of communal violence during the times of partition and the aftermath of it which tore apart the world of Lenny, a young Parsee girl growing up in the city of Lahore. She slowly awoke to the historical disaster and gained 'poisonous insights' as the multi-religious throng of her beautiful ayah's (maid servant) admirers began to indulge in internecine quarrels with regard to issues related to partition.

Ice-Candy Man is a penetrative study of minority complex—"the fear of being deprived, surpassed, losing out, threatened, dominated, suppressed, beaten down, exterminated and of losing one's identity and even life."[1] The sub-continent produced extremely talented rabble-rousers who specialised in turning a minority's grievances—real and imaginary—into a huge persecution complex. Some used it towards very narrow political ends. All the minorities dreaded that they would be hounded to death if Pakistan came into a reality. The Parsees of Lahore were aware of the fact that in the surcharged atmosphere where passions bound to rule reason that their survival was under threat. They knew that they, owing to the vulnerability and the lack of numerical strength, could not afford fighting a pitched battle against any section of society. Nor could they cherish any fond hope of siding any party because there was the possibility of "not one but two—or even three—new nations!"[2] Col. Bharucha warned Parsees that they should be very cautious lest they might find themselves championing the wrong side.

> If we're stuck with the Hindus, they'll swipe our business from under our noses...If we're stuck with the Muslims they'll convert us by the sword! And God can help us if we're stuck with the Sikhs! (p. 59)

The Parsees of Lahore were not 'stupid enough to court trouble' by backing up any community because they have something against everybody. They would not like to take an active part in politics because they dreaded that by 'jumping into the middle' they would be 'mangled into chutney.' They knew that 'it was not easy to be accepted into a country unless some ingenious norms for living with other communities were worked out.

> Let whoever rule! Hindu, Muslim, Sikh, Christian! We will abide by the rules of their land. (p. 39)

The novelist recounts the traditional story of the Parsees' arrival from Iran to India in the 8th century. An Indian prince sent a messenger to the Zoroastrian refugees fleeing Islamic expansion with a glass of milk, signifying that the Indian people were a united and homogeneous mixture that should not be tampered with. In response, the Parsees dropped a lump of sugar in the milk, saying that they would blend in easily and make the culture better and sweeter. It followed that they were granted a home in India because Parsees neither proselytised nor entered into politics.

The success of Parsees lies in the fact that by evolving certain workable norms and practical political strategies to live amiably with the majority, they tided over the problem of being driven out of Pakistan. It was they who did not bog down in minority complex, to a great extent and, therefore, they came out of identity politics'. They remained intact and prospered even under 'Muslim Moguls' simply because they continued to conduct their 'lives quietly' (p. 127). As 'a smart and civilized people' they wanted 'to sweeten the lives' of others. They did never engage themselves in proselytization; nor did they present 'threat to anybody.' It was resolved to a man that Parsees should be neutral in the tug-of-war among the three major communities, Hindu, Muslim and Sikh. The neutral attitude of the narrator character, Lenny had its roots in the racial psychology of the Parsees. Even the Parsees' children, Lenny and Adi, taking the cue from their elders, shouted themselves hoarse crying, 'Jai Hind! Jai Hind! Or 'Pakistan Zindabad'! depending on the whim or the allegiance of the principal crier.

In the final analysis this policy turns out to be very beneficial. While the Parsees were in harmony with the Muslims, the other minorities, Hindus and Sikhs, were uprooted from their homes and hearths and were subjected to atrocities unimaginable.

The Sikhs of Lahore, on the contrary, failed to come to terms with the Muslims. They kept on perpetuating old animosities with their policy of intolerance. Their verbal skirmishes with the Muslims bring out the fact that Sikhs' anger was occasioned by the fear complex. They dreaded that their community was confronting the danger of being blotted out and was on the brink of extinction. This feeling of insecurity did not make them sagacious and sane like Parsees but further aggravated the complex. As a result Mr. Singh and Sher Singh peeved at the Muslims at the slightest provocation and their arguments envenomed with spite which did not behove them well. Likewise, in the novel, *'The Sikh Soldier-Saint'*, Master Tara Singh was very vitriolic in his attack against the Muslims in Lahore.

> We will see how the Muslim swine get Pakistan! We will fight to the last man! We will show them who will leave Lahore! (pp. 133-134)

The tone and sense of the speech echoed Master Tara Singh who was very furious on seeing the flag being hoisted at the Assembly Hall, Lahore. He tore off the Muslim League flag into pieces and said:

> We cannot betray the Hindus...The time has come when the might of the sword alone shall rule. The Sikhs are ready. We have to bring the Muslims to their senses'. (Dr. Bakshish Singh Nijjar).

Speeches of this ilk can only spout venom and tarnish their image in the eyes of the Muslims. When the British pulled out of India, the Sikh community in Punjab province was caught in the land grab. Four and a half million Sikhs used to live in the part of Punjab region which is now in Pakistan. Today they are only 1,000. What happened to the Sikhs in 1947 in East Punjab was more like what is happening to the Muslims in Serbia today, long before the euphemism 'ethnic cleansing' came along (Shauna Singh). It is in the same darkness of morbidity that the Ice-Candy Man, a perfectly sane and fun-loving man, fraternising with Hindus of his menial class—has lost his reason and balance stabbing all and sundry and setting houses on fire as the train contained corpses of his religion.

The acrimonious speech can only invite more resentment, hatred and anger from the majority community. Having overheard the speech, the enraged Muslims made a battle cry.

> So? We'll play Holi—with—their blood! (p. 134)

Unlike the Parsees, the Sikhs failed to adopt a discreet policy fraternising with the Muslim League and sorting out the differences. This failure on their part cost them dearly—they were driven out of the Pakistan.

Bapsi Sidhwa shows a pattern of communal amity among the three communities. Underlying the basic unity among the various religions of India is the Hindu Ayah and her multi-religious throng of admirers. 'Hindu, Muslim, Parsi are...unified around her'. They are Masseur, Yousaf, Ice-Candy Man, Sher Singh, Moti, Hari and others. As the action of the novel moves forward, the novelist reveals the composite culture of rural areas by showing that Muslims' "relationships with the Hindus are bound by strong ties" (p. 56). They were dependent on each other. The Muslims of Pir Pindo, in obeisance to common ties, took part in Baisakhi festival.

On her maiden visit to Pir Pindo, a Muslim village, thirty miles off Lahore, Lenny found Muslims and Sikhs from the neighbouring village, Dera Tek Singh, sitting and sharing their concern about the worsening communal tensions in the cities. As the conversation continued, the novelist projects the contrasting communal outlook of town men with that of country folk. The Chaudhury, a Muslim of Pir Pindo, says:

> The country folk can afford to fight...We can't. We are dependent on each other, bound by our toil, by Mandi prices set by the Banyas—they're our common enemy—those city Hindus. To us villagers, what does it matter if a peasant is a Hindu, or a Muslim, or a Sikh? (p. 56)

A renowned sociologist, M.L. Darling, echoes the Chaudhry's remarks when he says: "A class of Hindu money-lenders had arisen in the Punjab which had enriched itself by exploiting the helpless peasantry."[3] The Punjabi peasants irrespective of their religions were being exploited by the Baniyas, their common enemy. In all provincial elections held in 1937, not Congress or Muslim League but the Unionist party which won at the hustings because the peasants were convinced that it could safeguard their interests. In fact, the roots of communal amity in rural Punjab went so deep that the members of the two communities were even ready to sacrifice their lives protecting each other. "If need be, we'll protect our Muslim brothers with our lives" (p. 56) said Jageat Singh. With the same vehemence the Chaudhry was quick to add "that every man in this village will guard his Sikh brothers with no regard for his own life" (p. 57). One gets the impression that the rural Punjab was an oasis of communal fraternity in the desert of communal frenzy ever expanding its tentacles to clutch the two communities in the cities. The villagers, despite buffetings from outside, put up a united effort to confront communal violence.

Partition is shown as the result of irreconcilability of the adamant and rash leadership which failed to understand that the malevolent nature of the differences would tell on the minds of ordinary people of India. Sharbat Khan rightly anticipated when he said to ayah thoughtfully:

> ...they are stirring up trouble for us all. (p. 76)

The novelist pulls the Congress leadership to pieces because the leadership failed at arriving some compromise with the League. The last promise for united India was held out by the Cabinet Mission rejected by the Congress leaders thereby "forcing of League to push for Pakistan" (p. 63). They refused to hear, or see that Jinnah had the backing of seventy million Indian Muslims. The Muslims believed that the Congress was very manipulative, activating, foul tactics by favouring 'some trumped-up Muslim party,' 'connived with Angrez to ignore the Muslim and manipulated one or two Muslims against the interests of the larger community'. These allegations against

Congress might be generated by the propaganda of Muslim League or have ring of truth. However, the Muslims were deeply convinced that the Congress leaders were after 'Jinnah's blood.' It was the sectarianism of the national leaders which wrought havoc on the lives of all.

The novelist does not spare the accountability of the British 'in inciting one against the other'. Mr. Singh was of the opinion that the British had long been supporting the Muslim League for some ulterior, self-seeking reasons. He bandied words with Inspector-General Rogers who threw his weight behind the Muslims. Rogers presented an excuse for Britishers' staying in India that all Indians would 'bloody fall at each other's throat' if 'they quit India.' He did not warn Indians in right earnest though his warning proved to be prophetic. He was one of many Britishers who believed in 'the Whiteman's burden.' Virtually since the founding of the National Congress, parallel with its growth through various stages, the official policy of active promotion of communalism was developed. 'Communalism was presented by the colonial administrators as the problem of the defence of minorities.' Looking from this perspective, Rogers appears to serve only as the mouthpiece of the British. Communalism was, in the words of the Government House Gardener, "the English's mischief...They are pastmasters in intrigue. It suits them to have us all fight" (p. 152). Instead of toning down the differences they played 'divide-and-rule monkey tricks' which led to partition.

The novelist clearly shows the hollowness of the two-nation theory. The division of Punjab, like the division of Bengal, was spurious because Punjabis were 'bound by strong ties' and were dependent on one another. The Sikh granthi said to the Chaudhry:

> Our villages come from the same racial stock. Muslim or Sikh, we were basically jats. We are brothers. (p. 56)

The novelist also shows the counterpart of the argument. In Lahore there was 'a group of smooth-skinned Brahmins' and their pampered male offspring who formed 'a tight circle of supercilious exclusivity.' This was, more or less, like that of

Parsees but the basic difference was that Parsees hobnobbed with each segment of the society. Lenny's mother used to invite and entertain many people from the city. Imam Din and the members of Lenny family exchanged pleasantries and religion was nothing to do with their social life. But Brahmins, being austere, could not even entertain such thoughts in their hearts. Worse, they could not stand the presence of Muslims and others. A Brahmin could not tolerate the mere 'shadow' of Muslims for it 'would violate his virtue'. When Lenny and Yousaf were going back home, they came upon a Brahmin who was taking meal 'out of a leaf-bowl'. The sanctity of caste was observed in such a way that even the sight of the Muslims was not only loathsome but also unholy. In this context what Sir Abdur Rahim has said is worthwhile: 'Any of us travelling for instance in Afghanistan, Persia, and Central Asia, among Chinese Muslims, Arabs and Turks, would at once be made at home and would not find anything to which we are not accustomed. On the contrary, in India we find ourselves in all social matters total aliens when we cross the street and enter that part of the town where our Hindu fellow townsmen live' (cited in Sir John Cumming, ed., *Political India* 1832-1932).

The dominant strain of the mood is reflected in Rahi Masoom Raza's novel, *Aadha Gaon* (Half-a-Village).

> "If Pakistan is not created the eighty million Muslims here will be made, and made to remain, untouchables."

On seeing them the Brahmin's face expressed the whole gamut of negative feelings, 'terror, passion and pain expected of a violated virgin' (p. 116), because they could not bear the presence of 'an outcast, an untouchable excrescence.'

> The vermilion caste-mark on his forehead glows like an accusing eye. He looks at his food as if it is infected with maggots. (pp. 116-117)

On seeing the leaf-bowl thrown away by the Brahmin, Yousaf's face was 'drained of joy, bleak, furious.' The repercussions it would set off cannot be underestimated especially when there were reasons to believe that one man's religion is another man's poison.' Jinnah asserted in 1941:

> ...a Muslim when he was converted, granted that he was converted more than a thousand years ago, bulk of them, according to your Hindu religion and philosophy, he becomes an outcast and he becomes a *mlecha* (untouchable) and the Hindus cease to have anything to do with him socially, religiously and culturally or in any other way? He, therefore, belongs to a different order, not only religious but social, and he has lived in that distinctly separate, antagonistic social order, religiously, socially and culturally. It is now more than a thousand years that the bulk of Muslims have lived in a different world, in a different society, in a different philosophy and a different faith."[4]

During the extreme phase of communalism, very broad generalizations were deduced on the premise of Hindus' exclusivity. They maintained unequivocally that Hindus and Muslims belonged to two separate nations, but not of 'the same racial stock.'

The novel shows the gradual emergence of the pattern of communal discord. When Masseur advised Sher Singh that it would be good for their community to cast their lot with one country rather than be divided into two halves thereby losing their 'clout in either place,' Sher Singh in an offensive tone, lashed out, saying:

> We can look out for ourselves...You'll feel our clout when the time comes! (p. 129)

The butcher, with all his professional mercilessness, called Sikhs 'a bloody nuisance.' Interestingly enough as the events rolled ahead with relentless speed, the group of ayah's admirers began to dwindle. Ayah was no longer just 'all-encompassing' as she had been but became 'a token', a Hindu.

> One day everybody is themselves—and the next day they are Hindu, Muslim, Sikh, and Christian. People shrink, dwindling into symbols. (p. 93)

The apathy of Ranna, a Muslim boy's acquaintances and friends, at a Baisakhi festival is symptomatic of the tension which the arrival of the Akalis in Dera Tek Singh had generated.

The pattern of communal harmony was replaced by the pattern of mutual distrust, suspicion and fear. With both the communities having taken up uncompromising positions the ensuing Holi festival would become 'a blood-soaked festival.'

The novelist clearly shows how religion was pressed into the service of communalism. Everybody began to lose his personal identity as they 'crammed into a narrow religious slot.' They became too religious and were carried away by a renewed devotional fervour. Ayah who was very frugal started expending 'a small fortune in joss-sticks, flowers and sweets on the gods and goddesses of the temples.' Imam Din and Yousaf, too, turned into 'religious zealots.' Religious appeal and religious symbols were used to garner support, to arouse religious hysteria and to whip up mass frenzy and ultimately all this brought about disastrous consequences.

What followed partition was the unbridled ventilation of the pent up rancour. While the Muslims of Pir Pindo that fell on the Indian side of the border were subjected to mass slaughter and rape by the marauding gangs of the Akalis, the Hindus and the Sikhs of Lahore underwent a similar harrowing experience.

> ...while the old city in Lahore crammed behind its dilapidated Moghul gates, burned, thirty miles away Amritsar also burned. (p. 207)

On his way to Pakistan from India, Ranna saw babies snatched from their mothers, smashed against the walls and their howling mothers were brutally raped and killed. He passed through the inferno of the trials and tribulations of refugees. The fate of Hindus who were forced to flee to India was not different, some were converted to Islam and Christianity.

The novelist objectively depicts the cataclysmic events. Ayah was abducted, raped and made a dancer in the Hira Mandi, the red light area of Lahore. It was a very traumatic experience for her because all this happened but with the active complicity of Ice-Candy Man, one of her admirers. Though he married her later, she was ' emptied of life and despairing.' When she was sent away to India on her own accord, Ice-Candy Man, now 'a truly harmless fellow' and a man of refined sensibility, 'disappeared across the Wagah border into India leaving the land he cherished for the sake of his Hindu beloved.

The Parsees, who till now, were on their guard, cautiously keeping themselves aloof from the communal conflagration, acted as the Messaiah of the other minorities, the Sikhs and the Hindus. Inspired by a feeling of humanism, they shook off their neutrality and 'wise passivity' and became the agents of a healing process.

What distinguishes Bapsi Sidhwa's *Ice-Candy Man* is 'the prism of Parsee sensitivity' through which the upheaval is depicted. It distills the love-hate relationship of the three communities through the consciousness and point of view of Lenny, a precocious Parsee girl. The flashback technique serves well as it captures the pace of actions and the tempo of it. However, the point of view is flawed on one account. She seems to tip the balance to Jinnah's side when she, all of a sudden, digresses.

> And today, forty years later, in films of Gandhi's and Mountbatten's lives, in books by British and Indian scholars, Jinnah, who for a decade was known as 'Ambassador of Hindu-Muslim Unity,' is caricatured, and portrayed as a monster. (p. 160).

Then she cited Sarojini Naidu's panegyric estimation of Jinnah's character! All this appears to be unnecessary and diffusing. The hatred and rancour between the two countries seem to be the legacy of partition and even beyond that and as such both countries are responsible. However, it may not be justified to allow this into the fictional framework.

Sidhwa successfully conveys the cataclysmic incidents of partition through Lenny's symbolic nightmares. The nightmare in which some men 'slice off a child's arm here and a leg there' and when the same men 'dismember' her she feels 'no pain but only an abysmal sense of loss,' symbolizes the impending vivisection of United India which was as cruel as the dismemberment of that child. Lenny's lack of pain, however, is suggestive of her community's indifference on account of its aloofness from the religio-political convulsion. The other nightmares foreshadowed the impending partition and dehumanized people turning on each other in a bewildering frenzy.

The novel, as Anita Desai puts it, 'astonishes by its novelty and freshness.' Certain phrases, for instance, 'absorbed in newsprint,' 'mud-packed roads' and others are fresh, brilliant and evocative. Here and there she appears pedanatic, for instance, when she uses 'hibiscus' for rose. Those are not too serious to cloud her credentials as a novelist. She is, indeed, an affectionate and shrewd observer and a born storyteller. To quote Anita Desai, 'there is no other writer I know on the sub-continent who combines laughter and ribaldry, a passion for history and for truth telling as Bapsi Sidhwa does in *Ice-Candy Man*.

REFERENCES

1. Bipin Chandra: *Communalism in Modern India*, (New Delhi: Vikas Publication Pvt. Ltd., 1987), 177.
2. Sidhwa, Bapsi: *Ice-Candy Man* (New Delhi: Penguin Books, 1989), p. 37. Further references to this text in this chapter will be cited parenthetically by page number.
3. Jagdev Singh: "*Ice-Candy Man:* A Perception on the Partition of India," *The Literary Criterion*, Vol. 27, 1993, p. 36.
4. Bipin Chandra: *Communalism in Modern India*, p. 158.

Final Appraisal

The sunrise of freedom on the sub-continent found millions done to death, mutilated or shamed, and tens of millions dispossessed of all that they had owned and cherished, and brutally tossed on both sides of the new border between India and Pakistan. It was a drama of degradation and shame, a drama of human decay, showing how the minds of the three communities were poisoned by the dogma of the two-nation theory.

Partition, a great national experience, generally serves as a great reservoir of literary material. The Indo-English novelists, Khushwant Singh, Chaman Nahal, Bisham Sahni and the Pakistani novelist, Bapsi Sidhwa, have treated partition comprehensively giving an artistic form to the holocaust. The novels on the whole weave a fine tapestry of various strands of partition.

Khushwant Singh's novel, *Train to Pakistan,* depicts how partition changes the very tenor of Mano Majrans, life and the transformation of the sleepy village one night of August 1947 into a cauldron of conflicting loyalists. A trainload of Sikhs, massacred by Muslims in Pakistan was cremated at Mano Majra. Consequently communal frenzy was in the air and the Sikhs wanted to settle scores by killing the Muslims setting off to Pakistan by train. But for Jugga the Muslims were all slaughtered. The novelist reveals that the barbarous incidents have a redeeming and humanising effect on even depraved men like Juggal Singh (and Hukum Chand, to some extent), who undergoes a complete metamorphosis. In performing the heroic deed to save the train carrying his beloved, a Muslim girl, along with other Muslims, Jugga becomes a sacrificial figure. His act redeems the abuse of religion that led to inhuman acts of violence.

In *Azadi*, Chaman Nahal offers 'an epic and psychological treatment' of the partition. Unlike the other novels, it probes into the motives of national leaders succumbing to partition under pressure. It scrutinizes, in detail, the causes of partition and the subsequent tragedy. To crown it all, it makes a very fine study of the psychological change effected by partition in the lives of Lala Kanshi Ram and others. With detached manner the novelist shows the accountability of the Hindus in India who were as much guilty as the Muslims on the other side of the border.

Tamas by Bhisham Sahni throws light on the cruel and foul acts of the persons who, in the garb of religion, perpetrated atrocities by whipping up communal frenzy. The novel unfolds the tragedies, caused by the slaughter of a pig thrown on the steps of the local mosque. The enraged Muslims began to massacre scores of the town's Hindus and Sikhs who, in turn, killed every Muslim they could find. Though the tide of communal frenzy was stemmed in, nothing could erase the awful memories etched on the minds of the survivors as all set off to grab power under the guise of peace-keeping. This novel offers an in-depth study pertaining to the two-nation theory and debunks the falsity of it stating that the 'roots' of Hindus, Sikhs and Muslims were the same.

Bapsi Sidhwa's *Ice-Candy Man* evokes the trauma brought about in the life of all communities in Lahore and at Pir Pindo. The acts of plunder, arson, abduction, mutilation and rape committed by all the communities on either side of the border reveal how false religiosity wrought havoc in the lives of all. It also exposes the hollowness of the two-nation theory and shows how communal amity embedded in the collective consciousness of the rural areas. The peasants of all communities knew for certain that they had 'come from the same stock' and were all basically Jats.' However, the novel is the study of minority complex, a mix of distrust, fear, and suspicion a resultant cause of the divide and rule of the British and rabid communalism. It offers incisive insights into the minds of different minorities who worked out their own strategies to face the impending partition. The novelist shows that unless some workable norms are chalked out to live in amity and peace with the majority, the chances of survival of the minorities are bleak. It is also a study of contrast between Parsees, who evolved a strategy to co-exist with the Muslims, and Sikhs who miserably failed owing to the lacuna in their approach of retaliation— 'an eye for an eye and a tooth for a tooth.' The denouement of the novel, and the defiling of the Ayah can be seen as reflecting the despoiling of a country. It is the truth—a recreation of Sidhwa's pungent memories of the partition tragedy. Lenny seems to be modelled on young Bapsi—the same age, the same religion and the same city and with the same disability. Perhaps the young Sidhwa's painful awareness of these women crammed into the genesis of the Ayah's story. The novel is a realistic portrayal born out of first-hand observation and experience.

The novels of partition do not exonerate the British. The British exploited the Hindu-Muslim feuds to their advantage, but they did not invent the enmity between the communities. It was already existent.

The novels, in the main, have castigated national leaders whose 'criminal short-sightedness and loss of nerve' brought about the vivisection of the country. All the leaders of united India—Gandhi, Nehru, Rajaji, Kripalani, Master Tara Singh and Jinnah—were held responsible because they were all at odds with one another in the times when unity, solidarity and concerted action were counted most. Barring a few passing references, there is no insight into the decisions that the leaders were compelled to take. Historical necessity is overt in *Azadi*.

All the novelists make it very clear that people belonging to the sub-continent were painfully conscious of their superfluous differences. They were completely oblivious to the act that they had common ancestors, history and heritage. Sahni says that Indians' 'roots were the same.' Bapsi Sidhwa declares that Indians 'came from the same stock' but Indians 'don't know history. They only live it.' Thus the novelists intend to convey that history has a moral. One of the major refrains in the novel is that in spite of the creation of the two nations a bond of oneness can clearly be discerned among the divided. Differences are always there whether religious, regional or others. It is wrong to make barriers out of them. Rather bridges have to be built as all hailed from 'the same stock.'

As India was poised and all set to achieve freedom communalists cutting across all parties and creeds began gloating over their religions thus directly responsible for the disaster. The 'bloody bunch of murdering fanatics' were members of national parties having 'one leg in the Congress boat and the other in the Hindu Mahasabha' or 'in the Muslim League.' The militant Sikh youth in *Train in Pakistan*, Abdul Ghani in *Azadi*, Murad Ali, Ranvir, Lakshmi Narain in *Tamas* and Sher Singh in *Ice-Candy Man* were all blatantly communal. Imbued with religious fervour they were ready to fall at each other's throats believing that they had a religious basis but they had not. What they posed as the problem was not a problem and what they suggested as a solution was not a solution. Barring *Tamas* where the instigator of violence, Murad Ali, towards the ending, posed as a lover of peace, the ending of all the other three novels terminates on a note of love and compassion. If evil and violence know no communal demarcation, neither do heroism and humanity. On watching the inhuman treatment given to Muslims in India—which had its counterpart in Pakistan—Kanshi Ram 'ceased to hate.' Likewise Juggal and Ice-Candy Man are transformed from utter rakes into compassionate men.

In fact, partition is such a vortex of communal issues that there is the possibility to be drawn helplessly to it to reflect one's idiosyncrasies and lack of correct judgement. But the novelists on partition, Khushwant Singh, Sahni, Nahal and Bipsi Sidhwa seem to be objective in the treatment of history and exhibit historical consciousness. Hard facts are not distorted at the expense of history. But there are certain episodes, for instance, Gandhi's appearance on the canvas of the novels, *Azadi* and *Ice-Candy Man*, do not have any historical authenticity.

Perhaps the novelists interpolate them in the fictional accounts with an intention to enliven interest in the plot. Such blending of the historical with the fictional entails to the exigencies of the plot of historical novels. 'They start from the particular, the historical and move to the universal.'

The structure of the novels seems to be compact and well-knit. The novelists seem to digress from the plot when they seek to convey the total insanity of partition-horrors. But for this lacuna, the novelists have imparted form and unity to the complicated and heterogeneous material. The various incidents, episodes and characters serve to illustrate the theme. There is a deeper and deeper probing into the same theme. It may be linked to a musical symphony in which the same emotion is probed into and studied from different angles.

In taking history into the realm of art, technique assumes a very significant tool in the hands of an historical novelist who is basically a creator, but his truth is poetic rather than statistical. All the novelists make use of point of view as a narrative mode as all of them were either the victims of partition or the spectators of it. Consequently, the tenor of the point of view, the tone and the atmosphere tend to be subjective and biased. However, they have not allowed the poignant memories to warp their sensibilities. The novelists seem to have succeeded in communicating to the readers a hint of the ghastliness and total insanity with commendable objectivity and without letting their novels degenerate into melodramas or sentimentalism. It seems that these novels have transcended sensationalism to a great extent and achieved the discipline of art.

Bibliography

PRIMARY SOURCES

I. Novels

Bapsi Sidhwa: *Ice-Candy Man*. New Delhi: Penguin Books, 1988.

—: *The Pakistani Bride*. New Delhi: Penguin Books, 1990.

—: *The American Brat*. New Delhi: Penguin Books, 1993.

Bhisham Sahni: *Tamas*. New Delhi: Penguin Books, 1987.

Chaman Nahal: *Into Another Dawn*. New Delhi: Sterling, 1977.

—: *My True Faces*. New Delhi: Vision Books, 1978.

—: *The English Queens*. New Delhi: Vision Books, 1979.

—: *The Crown and the Loincloth*. New Delhi: Vikas Publishing House Pvt. Ltd., 1981.

—: *The New Literatures in English*. New Delhi: Allied Publishers Private Limited, 1985.

—: *Sunrise in Fiji*. Ahmedabad: Allied, 1988.

—: *Jawaharlal Nehru as a Man of Letters*. New Delhi: Allied Publishers Limited, 1990.

—: *The Salt of Life*. Ahmedabad: Allied Publishers Limited, 1990.

—: *Azadi*. New Delhi: Allied Publishers Limited, 1993.

—: *The Triumph of the Tricolour*. New Delhi: Allied Publishers Limited, 1993.

—: *The Boy and the Mountain*. New Delhi: Allied Publishers, 1997.

Duggal, K.S.: *Twice Born Twice Dead*. New Delhi: Vikas Publishing House, 1979.

Hosain, Attia: *Sunlight on a Broken Column*. New Delhi: Arnold Heinemann, 1984.

Khushwant Singh: *Train to Pakistan*. Bombay: India House Pvt. Ltd., 1975.

Malgonkar Manohar: *A Bend in the Ganges*. New Delhi: Orient Paperbacks, 1964.

Narayan, R.K.: *Waiting for the Mahatma*. Mysore: Indian Thought Publication, 1969.

Rajan, Balachandra: *The Dark Dancer*. New Delhi: Arnold Heinemann, 1976.

II. Critical Works

Bipin Chandra: *Communalism in Modern India*. New Delhi: Vikas Publishing House Ltd., 1987.

Dhawan, R.K.: *Three Contemporary Novelists*. New Delhi: Classical Publishing Company, 1985.

Govinda Prasad Sarma: *Nationalism in Indo-Anglian Fiction*. New Delhi: Sterling Publishers Ltd., 1978.

Heehs, Peter: *India's Freedom Struggle*. New Delhi: Oxford University Press, 1988.

Mushirul Hasan: *Nationalism and Communal Politics in India*. New Delhi: Manohar Publishers, 1991.

Nicholson, Kai: *Presentation of Social Problems in the Indo-Anglian and Anglo-Indian Novel*. Bombay: Jaico Publishing House, 1972.

Sharma, K.K. and Johri, B.K.: *The Partition in Indian-English Novels*. Ghaziabad: Vimal Prakashan, 1988.

Sulochana Rangeya Raghava: *Sociology of Indian Literature*. Jaipur: Rawat Publications, 1987.

SECONDARY SOURCES

Abdul Kalam Azad, Maulana: *India Wins Freedom*. New Delhi: Orient Longman Ltd., 1988.

Badal, R.K.: *Indo-Anglian Literature*. Bareilly: Prakash Book Depot, 1975.

Basham, A.L.: *A Cultural History of India*. Delhi: Oxford University Press, 1975.

Bipin Chandra *et al.: India's Struggle for Freedom*. Delhi: Penguin Books, 1987.

Chirantan Kulshretha: "Khushwant Singh's Fiction" in *Considerations*, ed. Meenakshi Mukherjee. New Delhi: Allied Publishers Pvt. Ltd., 1977.

Collins, Larry and Lapierre, Dominique: *Freedom at Midnight*. New Delhi: Vikas Publishing House Pvt. Limited, 1975.

Fraser, G.S.: *The Modern Writer and His World*. Calcutta: Rupa and Company, 1961.

Grover, B.L. and Graves, S.: *A New Look at Modern Indian History*. New Delhi: S. Chand & Company Pvt. Ltd., 1998.

Kalinnikova, E.J.: *Indian English Literature*. Ghaziabad: Vimal Prakashan, 1982.

Krishna Rao, A.V.: *The Indo-Anglian Novel and the Changing Tradition*. Mysore: Rao and Raghavan, 1971.

Masood, Iqbal: *Dream Merchants, Politicians and Partition*. Delhi: HarperCollins, 1997.

Meenakshi Mukherjee: *The Twice-Born Fiction*. New Delhi: Heinemann Educational Books, 1971.

Melwani Murali Das: *Themes in Indo-Anglian Literature*. Barielly: Prakash Book Depot, 1977.

Menon, V.P.: *The Transfer of Power in India*. Princeton: Princeton University Press, 1967.

Naik, M.K., *et al.*: *Critical Essays on Indian Writing in English*. Dharwar: Karnataka University, 1979.

Naik, M.K.: *A History of Indian English Literature*. New Delhi: Sahitya Academy, 1982.

Narasimhaiah, C.D. (Ed.): *Fiction and the Reading Public in India*. Mysore: University of Mysore, 1967.

Paul Verghese, C.: *Problems of the Indian Creative Writer in English*. Bombay: Somaiya Publications Pvt. Ltd., 1971.

Perceival, Spear: *History of India*, Vol. 2, New Delhi: Penguin Books, 1998.

Prasad, Hari Mohan: *Response: Recent Revelations of Indian Fiction in English*. Barielly: Prakash Book Depot, 1983.

Radhakrishnan, S.: *The Hindu View of Life*. London: Unwin Books, 1960.

Raghavacharyulu: *The Critical Response*. Madras: Macmillan, 1980.

Raizada and Harish: *The Lotus and the Rose. (Indian Fiction in English* 1850-1947*)*. Aligarh: Faculty of Arts, A.M.U., 1978.

Sen, S.N.: *Modern India* (1765-1950). New Delhi: New Age International (P) Ltd., 2000.

Singh, R.S.: *Indian Novel in English*. New Delhi: Arnold Heinemann, 1977.

Sinha, N.K.: *Islam in India*. Patna: Khudha Bakhsh, Oriental Library, 1996.

Spencer, Dorothy, M.: *Indian Fiction in English*. Philadelphia: University of Pennsylvania Press, 1960.

Robert F. Spenser: *Religion and Change in Contemporary Asia*, Bombay: Oxford University Press, 1971.

Srinivasa Iyengar, K.R.: *Indian Writing in English*, 5th Edition. New Delhi: Sterling Publishers, 1985.

Tara Chand: *History of Modern India*. New Delhi: Publication Division, Ministry of Information and Broadcasting, 1974.

Verghese, C. Paul: *Problems of the Indian Creative Writer in English*. Bombay: Somaiya Publications, 1971.

Williams, H.M.: *Indo-Anglian Literature* (1800-1970). Madras: Orient Longman, 1976.

ARTICLES

Asnani, M. Syam: "A Study of the Novels of Manohar Malgonkar," *The Literary Half-Yearly*, XVI, January, 1975.

Atma Ram: "Interview with Khushwant Singh." *The Quest,* VII, October, 1993.

Batra Shakti: "Two Partition Novels." *Indian Literature,* XVIII, 1975.

Jagdev Singh: *"Ice-Candy Man*: A Perception on the Partition of India." *The Literary Criterion*, XXVII, Winter, 1993.

Jha, Rama: *"Azadi." Indian Literature,* XXI, 1975.

Mathur, O.P.: "The Novels of Chaman Nahal." *The Literary Half Yearly,* XX. 2, July, 1979.

Mushirul Hasan: "In Search of Integration and Identity." *Economic and Political Weekly*, XXII, November, 1993.

Patel Bhaichand: "Hindu Revivalists and Mimicking Islam Fundamentalism—Khushwant Singh and V.S. Naipal in Conversation." *Outlook,* May 8, 2000.

Punj, K. Balbir: "Results from the Lab." *Outlook*, December 30, 2002.

Shahane, A. Vasant: "Theme, Title and Structure in Khushwant Singh's *Train to Pakistan. The Literary Criterion*, IX, Winter, 1970.

Sharma, D.R.: "The Novels of Chaman Nahal. *The Journal of Indian Writing in English*, VII, January, 1979.

Sudha Sundaram: "Partition in Historical Fiction." *The Literary Criterion,* XXVIII, 1993.

Index

K

L

M

N

O

P

Q

R

S